London Kills

by the same author

MY BEAUTIFUL LAUNDRETTE and THE RAINBOW SIGN
(Screenplay)
SAMMY AND ROSIE GET LAID (Screenplay)
THE BUDDHA OF SUBURBIA (Novel)

Coming soon . . .

SELECTED PLAYS OF HANIF KUREISHI:
The King and Me, Outskirts, Borderline and Birds of Passage,
with an introduction by the author.

London Kills Me

HANIF KUREISHI

faber and faber
LONDON · BOSTON

First published in 1991
by Faber and Faber Limited
3 Queen Square London WC1N 3AU

Photoset by Parker Typesetting Service, Leicester
Printed in England by Clays Ltd, St Ives plc

British Library Cataloguing in Publication Data is available

ISBN 0-571-16566-4

Contents

Introduction

One day in the summer of 1989 I was followed along the Portobello Road by a boy of about twenty-one. He was selling drugs, as were many people around there, but this kid was an unusual salesman. For a start, he didn't mumble fearfully or try to intimidate. And he didn't look strong enough to shove a person in an alley and rob them. He was open-faced, young and direct; and he explained unasked the virtues of the drugs he was selling – hash, acid, Ecstasy – holding them up as illustration. As I vacillated, he explained lyrically about the different moods, settings and amounts appropriate for each drug.

We started to meet regularly. He liked to stand outside pubs, discussing people in the street. He'd think about which drug they'd prefer and wonder whether they'd purchase it from him, perhaps right now. Then he'd follow them.

He relished the game or challenge of selling, the particular use of words and the pleasures of conscious manipulation. He liked to con people too, selling them fake drugs, or promising to deliver the deal to them later. On the whole he was proud of his craft. He reminded me of the salesmen in Barry Levinson's *The Tin Men*. He was in a good position, that particular summer of love. He had a regular supply of drugs and there were plenty of customers. The kid knew there was a limitless market for what he had to sell. After all, drug-taking was no longer the sub-cultural preserve of those who knew its arcane language. Thirty years of a world-wide, sophisticated and mass culture, introduced by the Beatles, the Doors, Hendrix, Dylan and others, had spread the drug word, making certain drugs both acceptable and accessible. There was no combating it.

Now, new drugs like Ecstasy were especially in demand. Unlike LSD, for example, these were party drugs, weekend drugs, without noticeable after-effects. More usefully for the end of the 1980s, they were compatible with both holding down a full-time job and dancing in a field at four in the morning.

So most of the time the kid didn't much care if he made a sale or not. He wasn't desperate – yet. He moved from squat to squat and wasn't yet weary of being ejected, often violently, in the middle of the night. Anyhow, if things didn't go well he'd leave for Ibiza, Ecstasy Island, where many other young people were headed.

He loved to talk about himself, dwelling in vivid and creative detail on the fantastic adventures and tragedies of his life. Along with his drug dealing, these horrific and charming stories were his currency, his means of survival, enabling him to borrow money, ask a favour or stack up an ally for the future. So he told them to anyone who'd listen and to plenty of people who wouldn't. Again, it was a while before these stories became repetitive and self-pitying.

This kid's subject, his speciality let us say, or his vocation, was illegal drugs. He'd discuss enthusiastically the marvels and possibilities of Ecstasy, the different varieties of the drug and the shades of feeling each could induce. He looked forward to the new drugs he believed were being produced by hip chemists in San Francisco. This evangelical tone reminded me of the way LSD was talked about in the 1960s. I kept thinking that had the kid known about, say, the Victorian novel in the same detail, he'd have been set up for life by some university.

But a penchant for getting high and dealing to strangers was getting him banned from local pubs. He'd been stabbed, beaten up and slashed across the face. Sometimes he was picked up by the police, who 'disappeared' him into a police cell for two or three days, without charging him or informing anyone he was there. He'd been comforted and warned by social workers, probation officers and drug counsellors. Despite his glorious stories, he led a hard and painful life, not helped by the fact he was foolish as well as smart, indiscreet too, and without much foresight.

The intensity of this kid's life as he ran around the rich city, stealing, begging, hustling, was the starting point for *London Kills Me*. But his activities were bound up with the new music – Hip-Hop, House, Acid Jazz – and the entrepreneurial bustle surrounding it; the bands, record labels, shops, raves and warehouse parties organized in the squats, pubs and flats of Notting Hill. This reliable generational cycle of new music, fashion and attitude amounted to a creative resurgence reminiscent of the mid-1960s, and, of course, of the mid-1970s punk and New Wave, which was DIY music of another kind.

Notting Hill seemed an appropriate setting for the London

branch of what had been a mostly provincial and northern music movement. The North Kensington area had always had a large immigrant community: Afro-Caribbean, Portuguese, Irish, Moroccan. Many Spanish people, escaping fascism, had settled there. Its mixture of colours and classes was unique in London and it had a lively focal point, the Portobello Road and its market. Of the other previously 'happening' places in London, Chelsea had become a tourist's bazaar; and Soho had been overrun by the advertising industry. But like both these places, Notting Hill had cultural history. George Orwell was living in the Portobello Road in 1928 when he started to write the first pages of a play (one character of which was called Stone). Colin McInnes was part of the area's 1950s' bohemia. In the late 1960s the seminal *Performance* was set and filmed there. Not long afterwards Hockney took a studio in Powis Terrace. And in the 1970s the Clash's first album featured a montage of the 1976 carnival riot on its cover.

In 1959, after seeing Shelagh Delaney's *A Taste of Honey*, Colin McInnes wrote: 'As one skips through contemporary novels, or scans the acreage of fish-and-chip dailies and the very square footage of the very predictable weeklies, as one blinks unbelievingly at "British" films, it is amazing – it really is – how very little one can learn about life in England here and now.'

A few years later his wish began to be granted. There developed a tradition, coming out of Brecht and stemming from the Royal Court and the drama corridor of the BBC, of plays, series and films which addressed themselves to particular issues – unemployment, or racism, or housing – usually seen through the inescapable British framework of class. This work was stimulated by the idea of drama having a use or purpose, to facilitate society's examination of itself and its values, creating argument and debate about the nature of life here and now. Many actors, writers, directors and designers were trained to see their work in this way.

Out of this came the brief resurgence of low-budget British films in the mid-1980s. The myriad tensions of life under Thatcher were irresistible to writers and film-makers. Here was the challenge of a Conservatism that had, at last, admitted to being an ideology. Here were ideas – at a time when the Left had none. The cultural reply was not presented in the language of social realism; both victims and heroes of the class struggle were eschewed. These were popular films wishing to reach a large audience hungry for debate about the new age of money and what it meant.

One issue rarely discussed in this way has been drug use. It's an odd omission as, since the mid-1960s, in most towns and cities of a good deal of the world, young people have been using illegal drugs of various kinds. There hasn't been much fiction about this subject and the life that goes with it; and remarkably little hard information about drugs is provided to people, though cautionary and scary stories are propagated in the vain hope of frightening them.

Although drugs are fundamental to the story, *London Kills Me* was never primarily 'about' drug use. The film is concerned mainly with the lives of the characters. It was always, for me, a story about a boy searching for a pair of shoes in order to get a job as a waiter in a diner. Even so, when we were seeking out money for the movie – and it was not expensive – there was criticism from potential backers about the drug use in the film. They were worried that they might be accused of 'recommending' drugs.

The text published here is the film's fifth draft, the version we began with on the first day of shooting. Some scenes we filmed exactly as written but others developed as we rehearsed. Some just changed in front of the camera. A certain amount of the dialogue was made up by the actors.

Many films and more television plays are planned meticulously before they start shooting. There are shot-lists and story-boards for every second of the film. The director, cameraman, producer, art director and assistants work out the camera- and actor-moves on scale plans before shooting begins. Making the film itself is then a process of reproduction. It isn't the necessary requirements of planning that make this way of working seem objectionable. It is the expectation or hope of safety and security that is deadening, the desire to work without that moment of fear – when you really don't know how to go on – and therefore to create without utilizing the unexpected.

I've never written in a planned way and I tried, even as a first-time director, not to work like this. It would bore me to know in the morning what exactly I'd be doing in the afternoon. And Stephen Frears, whose advice I sought, said it was 'fatal' to work to a strict plan. Having worked with him twice as a writer, I didn't want to have any less enjoyment than he clearly had when shooting a film.

Much to my surprise, having written the film and then being in the powerful position of being able to direct it too, I felt less possessive about my dialogue and the shape of the script than I had when someone else was in charge. In the end, all I clung to was the story, to getting that, at least, in front of the camera.

The script of *London Kills Me* was only ninety pages long: a tight little film without much wastage. I couldn't see there'd be much to lose in the editing. I thought every scene was essential and in the best place. We wouldn't waste a lot of time shooting material we'd never use. Editing would be relatively simple. So I was pretty surprised when the first rough assembly of the film was over two and a half hours long. I found myself in the odd position of having written a film and then shot it – and still I didn't know what sort of movie I was supposed to be making, what the tone was to be. The editing, like writing, I realized, would also become a form of exploration and testing of the material. It was all, even this, an attempt to tell a story by other means.

Hanif Kureishi
London, April 1991

The cast and crew of *London Kills Me* are as follows:

CLINT	Justin Chadwick
MUFFDIVER	Steven Mackintosh
SYLVIE	Emer McCourt
DR BUBBA	Roshan Seth
HEADLEY	Fiona Shaw
LILY	Eleanor David
STONE	Alun Armstrong
TOM-TOM	Stevan Rimkus
BURNS	Tony Haygarth
FAULKNER	Nick Dunning
BIKE	Naveen Andrews

Director of Photography	Ed Lachman
Production Designer	Stuart Walker
Stills Photographer	Jacques Prayer
Music Consultant	Charlie Gillett
Music Composers	Mark Springer and Sarah Sarhandi
Editor	Jon Gregory
Associate Producer	David Gothard
Executive Producer	Tim Bevan
Producer	Judy Hunt
Director	Hanif Kureishi

A Working Title Production.
Distributed by Manifesto.

London Kills Me was filmed on location in London during 1991.

London Kills Me

Hanif Kureishi was born in 1954 and brought up in Bromley,
Kent. He read philosophy at King's College, London, where he
started to write plays. In 1981 he won the George Devine Award
for *Outskirts*, and in 1982 was appointed Writer in Residence at
the Royal Court Theatre. In 1984 he wrote the screenplay for *My
Beautiful Laundrette*, which subsequently received an Oscar
nomination for Best Original Screenplay. His second film, also
directed by Stephen Frears, was *Sammy and Rosie Get Laid*. His
novel, *The Buddha of Suburbia*, won The Whitbread Prize for
best first novel in 1991. *London Kills Me* is his first feature as a
director.

EXT. STREET. DAY
As the credits roll we see CLINT *on the street:* CLINT *is white,
fair-haired, pretty, thin, vain, with much charm and nerve. He suffers
from eczema all over his body – skin broken and cracked – so he's
perpetually scratching himself and twitching.
He's carrying a large bottle of mineral water which he uncaps. He
produces a toothbrush and toothpaste from the top pocket of his jacket
and using the bottled water he cleans his teeth.
Then he produces a dirty old piece of soap from his pocket and once
more using the water, he washes his face and hands.
Finally he wets his hair.
Cut to:*

EXT. STREET. DAY
CLINT *walking purposefully through the city.
Cut to:*

EXT. STREET. DAY
Now CLINT'*s checking his look in the reflecting glass of the diner. He
thinks he looks fine: he's had a wash, and his clothes, at this point,
are pretty good.
Cut to:*

EXT. GOLBORNE ROAD. DAY
CLINT *walking purposefully through the city. We see* HEADLEY,
HEMINGWAY *and* TOM-TOM *on street.
Cut to:*

EXT. VERNON YARD. DAY
CLINT *in a secluded doorway. He's smoking a spliff as he takes out a
roll of money and hides it in different bits of his clothing, including his
shoes and socks. He does this quickly, as if practised at it.
Cut to:*

EXT. STREET. DAY
CLINT *on the phone in the street, a tower of ten pences on the box, a*

3

wretched piece of paper in hand, with phone numbers on it.
A young girl comes by and puts her prostitute's calling card in the glass
booth. Very businesslike. CLINT *tries to talk to her as she walks away,*
as well as talking into the phone.
Cut to:

EXT. STREETS. DAY
CLINT *walking purposefully through the city.*

EXT. STREET. EVENING
We see CLINT *on the the bridge, walking. He stops to tie his*
shoe-laces. Picks up something from the ground, pockets it. He's
always alert in this way.
SYLVIE *has seen him and she watches him doing this, amused by him.*
She goes to him. They haven't seen each other for a while. They greet
each other warmly. MUFFDIVER *is hanging out in doorway, watching*
them. MUFFDIVER *is a skinny little kid of nineteen, a wiry dirty boy*
without CLINT*'s charisma. But he's tougher than* CLINT, *more*
determined and more organized. He's a drug-dealer and starting to
move into the big time.
SYLVIE: How you doing, Clint?
CLINT: Good, good. Not too bad. Looking for a job.
SYLVIE: Now?
CLINT: No. Come with me.
SYLVIE: Where, little Clint?
CLINT: Little rave.

EXT. MOROCCAN CAFÉ. DAY
They walk past the Moroccan café where the Moroccans sip mint tea.
They walk past the Rasta Information Centre. The street is busy and
lively, colourful and mixed. Music comes from various cafés and
shops. There is music on the street constantly. They talk and laugh,
arm in arm, though CLINT *never relaxes and glances around*
continually, both out of nervousness and interest.
Across the street MUFFDIVER *is standing in a doorway.*
MUFFDIVER: (*To himself*) Tsa-Tsa, she's nice.
    (*He knows* CLINT *well.* CLINT *works for him. They're very old*
    friends. MUFFDIVER *goes across to them.*)
    Wha' 'appening?
CLINT: Going to a rave, later.

4

MUFFDIVER: (*Looking at* SYLVIE) Yeah? Something 'appening.
CLINT: Sylvie 'appening. Sylvie. Muffdiver.
SYLVIE: Pleased to meet you, Muffdiver. Always nice to make new
friends.
(MUFFDIVER *looks at* SYLVIE. *She is less interested in him than
he in her. He stares at her, fascinated. Meanwhile* CLINT *calls out
to* BURNS, *who is sipping tea at a table inside the Moroccan place.*
CLINT *goes inside.*)

INT. MOROCCAN CAFÉ. DAY
CLINT: Burns! Burns! Yo, man, rave.

EXT. MOROCCAN CAFÉ. DAY
And BURNS, *a fat Scotsman in his fifties, comes paddling into the frame,
eating. As the four of them walk,* MUFFDIVER *nudges* SYLVIE *and she
does a double-take as he pulls a string of handkerchiefs out of his mouth.*
MUFFDIVER: Squad.
(*Two plainclothes policemen pass in front of them. Automatically
they cool down, their faces becoming masks.*
When the men have gone, CLINT *gives an Indian whoop.* SYLVIE
looks at him and laughs.)

INT. HOUSE PARTY. NIGHT
*A party. The place jumping. A mixed, black and white, party. Music.
Dope. Dancing. Everything you'd expect.*
CLINT *and* MUFFDIVER *are accompanied by* BURNS. *We see them
swing into the room and greet people. They're obviously well-known
there.*
A couple of kids go to BURNS *and ask him questions. He's dealing. He
turns away with them, putting his hand in his pocket.*
MUFFDIVER *experimentally puts his arm around* SYLVIE *and whispers
in her ear. Then he kisses her cheek. She is surprised by his attention.*
CLINT *is surprised by* MUFFDIVER's *move, but as usual he's concerned
with other things, always curious.*
Cut to:

INT. ANOTHER PART OF HOUSE. NIGHT
Later. MUFFDIVER *leaning back against a wall, stoned, with a joint.*
CLINT *and* SYLVIE *talking in another part of the room.* BURNS *dancing
with a girl, enjoying himself.*

5

A young black MAN *goes to* MUFFDIVER. *They greet each other, their faces close.*
MUFFDIVER: Buyin'?
MAN: Na.
MUFFDIVER: Sellin'?
MAN: I hear you lookin' for Mr G. You ready for Mr G I reckon. But he want to know you properly organized and everything.
MUFFDIVER: Yeah, I appreciate.
MAN: OK, I'll fix it. (*Indicates* CLINT.) Who that geezer?
MUFFDIVER: That's Clint. Why, he in trouble again?
> (*The* MAN *winks and moves away.* MUFFDIVER *is alarmed as the* MAN *moves towards* CLINT. CLINT *gets up. The* MAN *takes* CLINT *away from* SYLVIE. *The* MAN *indicates to* MUFFDIVER *to keep out of it.* MUFFDIVER *sits with* SYLVIE.)

INT. BARE ROOM. NIGHT
The MAN *throws* CLINT *into a bare dark room, maybe with just a mattress on the floor. Pots of paint etc. There are two other guys in the room now, one* BLACK, *one* WHITE, *all young and threatening.* CLINT *backs away, terrified, whimpering.*
MAN: You owe me some money, Mr Clint, man, from that time you are recalling now, right?
> (CLINT *is furious with himself for getting into this shit. His hands are shaking as he empties his pockets. Then, after a nod from the* MAN, *he removes a fiver from the collar of his shirt. The* MAN *takes the money but is unimpressed by it.*)
That all you carryin', boy? You strip.
WHITE MAN: Yeah.
CLINT: I got nothin'.
> (CLINT *removes his clothes to his underpants. The* MAN *nods and the pants come off too. The men laugh at* CLINT's *puny eczema-ridden body. They search his clothes. Suddenly one of them holds up money.*)
WHITE MAN: In the shoe!
BLACK MAN: In the shoe? Chew the shoe, chew the shoe, boy! Do him!
> (*They all close in on* CLINT. *Suddenly one of the men hits him across the legs with a pool cue. He cries out.*)

6

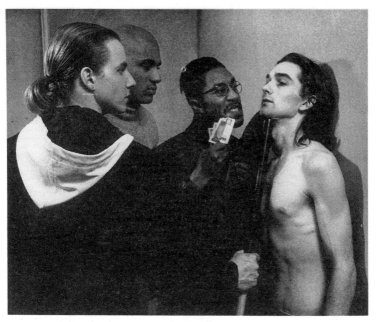

INT. HOUSE PARTY. NIGHT
Quick cut to the loud music of the house. Here MUFFDIVER *is talking*
to SYLVIE. BURNS *is eating a plate of food.*
MUFFDIVER: I've seen you around the pub and in the street,
Sylvie, but I've never talked to you, though I've wanted to.
For a long time.
(*Pause. He's getting nowhere with her.*)
Shall I tell you something? Burns is quite fat. He had his
stomach sewn up, to stop him eating. But the bit that was left
has expanded. Or maybe the stitches burst, I can't remember
what he told us. A person's stomach is only the size of your
fist, you know. But it's elastic.
(*Pause.*
He pulls a lighted cigarette out of her ear. She doesn't respond.
He pulls a lighted match from the other. She smiles.)
SYLVIE: Where's that boy?
MUFFDIVER: You're right about him. He needs us, his friends.
That's why I'm getting us a place. Need somewhere yourself.
(*She is interested in him.*)

7

Why don't you come with me? Come on. We'll go somewhere. How about it?

EXT. PARTY HOUSE. NIGHT
MUFFDIVER *and* SYLVIE *walk down the steps of the house, or stand at the top of the steps.*
MUFFDIVER: What sort of music do you like? I like House and Hendrix. The three Hs are for me, eh? That was a dread party. Clint's idea. What a fool.
Cut to:

EXT. STEPS UNDER HOUSE. NIGHT
We see CLINT, *naked and covered in mud, under the steps, shivering but then laughing as he hears his friend* MUFFDIVER'S *pretentious rap to the aloof* SYLVIE.

EXT. PARTY HOUSE. NIGHT
MUFFDIVER *is about to put his arm around* SYLVIE *when* CLINT *rises up.* SYLVIE *goes to him.*
SYLVIE: Clint, Clint, for God's sake, get up! Are you hurt? We didn't know where you'd gone.
CLINT: I like fresh air, innit. Sylvie, I tell you, I'm finished with this shit life. This eating shit fuckin' life. I'm really getting a job.
MUFFDIVER: When?
CLINT: Tomorrow. Meet me at ten fifteen outside the diner and I'll show you how to conduct an interview with an employer.
SYLVIE: Don't be hasty, Clint. Things are not that bad.
MUFFDIVER: And you'll have to find some clothes first, man.
CLINT: It was smoky in there, so I flogged my clothes to a man with no trousers.
SYLVIE: Have a heart, Muffdiver.
MUFFDIVER: He brings these things on himself. Do they happen to me?
CLINT: You've got to know. It's my birthday. Now, at this moment in the whole history of the world I'm twenty years old.
SYLVIE: Say happy birthday, Muffdiver.
(*She nudges* MUFFDIVER *to congratulate* CLINT. *He murmurs a few words.*)

8

MUFFDIVER: Happy birthday, Clint.
>   (MUFFDIVER *makes a gesture towards* SYLVIE, *and she*
>   *responds.* CLINT *sees they're together now. He feels excluded. He*
>   *moves away, hurt.*)
CLINT: I'm just glad I spent it with friends.
>   (*He walks away naked.*)
MUFFDIVER: (*To* SYLVIE) They won't let him into the
>   Subterrania like that. They've got a very strict door policy.

EXT. STREET. NIGHT
A shopping street at three in the morning. CLINT *walks naked along*
the street. BIKE, *a young Indian kid (on his bicycle) circles around*
him, eating a Chinese takeaway.
CLINT: I'm gonna live an ordinary life from now on. I know it's
>   possible.
>   (*Two transvestites,* FAULKNER *and another, pass* CLINT *and*
>   *glance coolly at him.*)
FAULKNER: Hi Clint. Good start.

EXT. TRASH BAGS ON STREET. NIGHT
Another part of Notting Hill. CLINT *is going through a pile of plastic*
rubbish bags bursting with puked Chinese dinners. But he's found a
pair of trousers, and – hey presto – a filthy pair of workman's boots.
These are big boots.
CLINT *turns and sees an extraordinary apparition. A large black*
tramp, in rags, wild hair, covered in filth, carrying an immense
number of bags (some of which are tied to his body), moves closer and
closer to CLINT, *his eyes fixed on him.*

EXT. JEWELLER'S DOORWAYS. DAWN
Three or four young people are sleeping, wrapped in cardboard,
blankets and papers, one of them cowering behind umbrellas. CLINT
has spent the night here. He wakes up. He flattens his hair with spit.
Then he sneaks a pair of socks from the person behind the umbrella.
BUSY BEE *is awake, shaking out a jumper.* CLINT *watches him.*
BUSY BEE *notices* CLINT *and watches him warily.*
CLINT: I need to lend that jumper.
BUSY BEE: What's wrong with *The Times*?
>   (*And he throws* The Times *at him.*)
CLINT: You don't understand, Busy Bee. I got a job interview

this morning. Big interview ting.

BUSY BEE: What drugs you gonna give me, Mr Clint Eastwood?

>(CLINT *grabs the jumper and runs away with it.* BUSY BEE *chases him,* CLINT *laughing and running, pulling on the jumper.*)

INT. DINER. DAY

We're in a busy hamburger diner at lunchtime. This is an upmarket place frequented mainly by well-off media types. The tables are full, the activity frantic. A young well-dressed young woman snaps her fingers and calls sharply to a waiter.

A young black waitress, MELANIE, *hurries over to her. The woman speaks to* MELANIE.

At another table two SMART WOMEN *are working – looking through a pile of papers and files, and discussing them. One of them drops a piece of paper.*

CLINT, *who we now see is observing all this, just standing there, nips over and picks up the papers. He holds on to the document, gaining the* WOMAN'S *attention. His clothes are too big and dirty and he sticks out in the restaurant.*

There is, behind the bar, throughout this film, an incredibly flash barman, mixing complicated cocktails in a particularly theatrical way. The SMART WOMAN *smiles at* CLINT. *He whispers at her.*

CLINT: Need any washing done?

SMART WOMAN: What?

CLINT: Car cleaned? Washing by hand. Gardening by hand.

>(*She glances at her friend and they both laugh.*)

>Need any black hash? Proper ting.

>(*They're interested, after a nodded consultation, but now* HEMINGWAY, *the American manager in a suit and open-necked shirt, comes out, looks for* CLINT, *and seeing him, takes his arm and examines his face with natural affection and interest.* HEMINGWAY *is very cool, and sees everything about a person immediately.*)

HEMINGWAY: You Clint, yeah?

>(CLINT *struggles to cope, to appear straight and normal.*)

CLINT: Yeah. Mr Clint. How you doing? Do you think you can do like what your friend promised me?

HEMINGWAY: What promise did my friend make to you, exactly?

CLINT: Get me a job here. She say the manager a wally but you know the manager intimately close, she say.

HEMINGWAY: I am the manager, Mr Hemingway.

CLINT: All this is you? Cool photos. Sturdy chairs. Top people sitting.

(*He winks at the two* SMART WOMEN.)

HEMINGWAY: OK, OK. Underneath everything you might be a good boy. Work experience? (*Pause.*) What work have you done?

(CLINT *thinks for a while, looking at the waitress flying spectacularly about, the barman mixing drinks.*)

CLINT: But I could pick up one of them plates.

(*And he goes to the* SMART WOMEN'*s table and starts removing their plates, piling them up on his arm.*)

HEMINGWAY: All right, OK, you gotta start somewhere. It's decent work when you learn how to do it.

(*He takes* CLINT *aside.*)

Just don't mess me around, OK? Come back Tuesday morning. I feel someone's gonna walk out on me that day. Clean yourself up. And do one thing. Just one, right?

(*We pan down* CLINT's *legs to his boots. We see, with*
HEMINGWAY, *his disgusting boots.*)
You understand, don't you, that I can't have footgear like
that in my place. There is disease there. Film people come in
here. So, no new shoes – no job. No job – back on the street.
Back on the street – (*and he shrugs*) – shit!
(CLINT *nods, glances at the window to make sure* MUFFDIVER *is
outside watching all this, which he is. When he sees* CLINT
looking at him he turns away, not acknowledging him. CLINT
puts out his hand.)
CLINT: Put it there, Mr Hemingway. I wish all my problems were
of that cool order. See you Tuesday.
(HEMINGWAY *watches him go. As he goes,* CLINT *smiles at*
MELANIE, *who smiles back at him. He stops for a moment to
talk to her, but sees* HEMINGWAY *looking at him. He goes.*)

EXT. STREET. DAY
CLINT *strides cheerfully out of the restaurant.* MUFFDIVER *is waiting
outside for him and runs to catch up with* CLINT *as he walks
confidently away from the diner.*
CLINT: Start Tuesday. Everything's A-1 fixed up. There's just
one thing I need –
MUFFDIVER: Clint, Clint –
CLINT: A pair of shoes. Good shoes. Great shoes.
MUFFDIVER: The job's out then. It's a dead-end, it's –
CLINT: All these people got shoes. Look. Hush Puppies, DMs,
sandals, brogues, loafers, high-tops. Give me a single reason
why I shouldn't get some.
MUFFDIVER: Because you a fool.

EXT. PUB. DAY
*The two friends are on the street and they know a lot of people. The
black kids outside the pub, greet them.* CLINT *calls out to a girl in the
street.*
CLINT: Hey Yvonne, wha' 'appenin'? Wanna buy any E? Any
bush? What about a pair of shorts?
(*And he pulls a pair of shorts out of somewhere. She shakes her
head, laughing.*)

EXT. SHOE SHOP. DAY

Then CLINT *is standing outside a shoe shop. He's trying on a strong black boot which he's taken down from a display. He does a little dance wearing the one new boot. It fits and he's celebrating. The shop assistant, a young white-faced girl in black, her long hair standing straight up, watches him suspiciously.* CLINT *delicately puts the shoe back.* MUFFDIVER *is in the background.*

EXT. STREET. DAY

Later. CLINT *and* MUFFDIVER *walking quickly, heading towards a squat that's been recommended to them.*

MUFFDIVER: Fuck me? Fuck me, why, for fuck's sake?

CLINT: Because what's my life doing?

MUFFDIVER: Clint –

CLINT: It's coming together. I can make it without you.

MUFFDIVER: Yeah, sure, where's the shoes?

CLINT: You can't put me down, because the shoe is due.

MUFFDIVER: Yeah, like my arse is due. You got no money for shoes.

CLINT: I'll work for you until Tuesday.

MUFFDIVER: No. You don't even work for me now.

CLINT: What?

MUFFDIVER: You're not professional.

CLINT: And there's my new home. Our office suite. It's ready for business occupation, right? We're swinging over there now, yeah? It's a palace you said –

MUFFDIVER: Yeah, I said.

CLINT: I had to sleep out last night, Muffdiver.

MUFFDIVER: There's Headley.

EXT. STREET. DAY

They look across the street where HEADLEY *is walking along, a TV interviewer with her, a cameraman and sound guy in front of her. She talks eloquently about the area, indicating people and shops. As the crew moves backwards, out of a doorway comes the black tramp in rags, lumbering into shot.*

They stop shooting. HEADLEY *sees* CLINT *and* MUFFDIVER *and indicates for them to come over.*

CLINT: I don't wanna see her.

MUFFDIVER: She's business, man.

CLINT: She's always wanting.

MUFFDIVER: She's drug business, man.

    (MUFFDIVER *leads* CLINT *into the gallery*.)

INT. GALLERY. DAY

MUFFDIVER: Let's look at some artwork for the new place.

    (CLINT *and* MUFFDIVER *have joined a gallery opening. Young smart people holding glasses. Wealthy attractive people.*

    MUFFDIVER *looks at all this with much interest and envy.*

    CLINT *and* MUFFDIVER *mingle.* CLINT *takes a drink from a passing tray and hands one to* MUFFDIVER.

    MUFFDIVER, *cool and distant, doesn't take much notice of* CLINT, *who's always going on at him*.)

CLINT: This squat, we're not going to be let down. Is it definite? I can't be a waiter and sleep in the gutter.

MUFFDIVER: What about Sylvie? Is she definite?

CLINT: What? (*He's amazed*.) With you? With Sylvie? You?

MUFFDIVER: Don't keep saying her name like that. How d'you know Sylvie anyway?

CLINT: Sylvie. I've known her so long I can remember when she didn't drink.

MUFFDIVER: How come I haven't seen her before, then?

    (*A woman is beside* MUFFDIVER, *looking for a light.* CLINT *steals a gold lighter from the table and lights the cigarette. He puts the lighter in* MUFFDIVER's *pocket*.)

CLINT: Sylvie was in the drug rehab.

MUFFDIVER: But she's back on. (*Pause. He can't tear his eyes away from the surroundings.*) These people. Tsa-Tsa. They got clothes, cars, houses –

CLINT: Shoes.

MUFFDIVER: Maisonettes. Everything.

    (MUFFDIVER *walks decisively out of the place, as if he's decided what he must do with his life from now on.* CLINT, *as always the deputy, walks out behind him, stealing a bottle of champagne and putting it under his jacket as he goes*.)

EXT. BACK OF SQUAT. DAY

CLINT *and* MUFFDIVER *stand at the back of a five storey London house, looking up at the rear of the building.*

MUFFDIVER: Tom-Tom said it's a whole luxury place. The

owner's done a runner – he's some big criminal. We've
probably got three months of total mod-cons.

CLINT: Great, total con-mods.

MUFFDIVER: Okay, in through the window.

(CLINT *removes his jacket. As he does so, he talks to the world in
general.*)

CLINT: The shoe is due. The new shoe is overdue. (*To*
MUFFDIVER.) Which floor?

MUFFDIVER: Top.

(CLINT *vacillates, moves backwards.* MUFFDIVER *grabs him
and shoves him towards the building.*)

I'll keep a sharp look-out!

Cut to:

EXT. BACK TO SQUAT. DAY
Now CLINT *is clambering up the drainpipe, about half-way up the
side of the tall building. Very dangerous.* CLINT *hears a popping noise
and looks down to see* MUFFDIVER *swigging from a bottle of
champagne.* MUFFDIVER *gives him the thumbs-up and indicates for
him to continue upwards.*

Cut to:

EXT. BACK OF SQUAT. DAY
CLINT *has climbed up to the floor below the top one, and is clinging perilously to the drainpipe. From his point of view we get a high view over London. Then he turns back to the face of the building and looks into a large room.*

INT. SUFI CENTRE. DAY
This is the Sufi Centre. About twenty people holding hands in a circle and moving slowly clockwise. In the middle of the circle are four people whirling and chanting as they move.
The Sufi whirlers are all white, apart from two black girls. Mostly it's young hippyish women in casual clothes.
Outside the circle is DR BUBBA, *an Indian, instructing them what to do and clouting a drum which he holds under his arm. An old man, whirling, wearing a bow-tie, opens his eyes and sees* CLINT *suspended outside the window. He does a double-take. Then he accepts that he is having a vision and he puts his hands together and acknowledges* CLINT *as an angel, since* CLINT *has, from his point of view, developed wings.*

EXT. BACK OF SQUAT. DAY
CLINT *scrambles upwards.*
Cut to:

EXT. BACK OF SQUAT. DAY
CLINT *is right at the top of the house, but the drainpipe is starting to come away from the wall.* CLINT *tries frantically to grab at things but there's nothing near by. He holds on to a grating for a few seconds but it pulls out of the wall and crashes to the ground, just missing* MUFFDIVER *who yells angrily up at* CLINT.
CLINT *looks down. He feels certain he's going to die. He is terrified. He knows he can't climb down the breaking drainpipe.*
CLINT: Help me MUFFDIVER, help me, man!
 (*He manages to look down at* MUFFDIVER *standing there.* MUFFDIVER *genuinely distressed and confused.*)
MUFFDIVER: What can I do?
CLINT: Call the police!
 (CLINT *watches* MUFFDIVER *who takes a few paces away, but returns and indicates complete helplessness.*)
Cut to:

EXT. BACK OF SQUAT. DAY

CLINT *has grabbed another pipe above the window frame. He pulls himself up and swings around the side of the building, where there's a balcony. He clambers on to the balcony. The glass doors to the flat are locked. He smashes one of the windows with a brick, cutting himself. But he lands on the leopard-skin carpet, covered in blood.*

INT. LIVING ROOM OF SQUAT. DAY

CLINT, *cut and bleeding, walks around the squat, wiping the blood off himself with a white towel.*
The squat has clearly been burgled a few times: the TV and stereo ripped out, and records and clothes and rubbish strewn about the place.
CLINT *walks from room to room, taking in the thick carpets, glass tables (cracked or smashed), and broken pin-ball machine. The living room is a big space. There is a bar but all the bottles are empty or smashed.*
CLINT, *as he walks about, is more and more pleased with what he sees, grunting and whistling his approval.*

INT. SQUAT. BEDROOM. DAY

CLINT *in the master bedroom, lying on the bed.*
He discovers switches beside the bed which operate the curtains; these move furiously back and forth. He enjoys this for a while. Then he fiddles with the lights in the room, which go off and on, dimming and brightening. He's really like a child now, unable to believe his good fortune.
Finally he hits another button and a huge TV cabinet opens. A shelf comes out, on which there's a plate of rotting food.
Cut to:

INT. CLINT'S BEDROOM. DAY

Now CLINT *is trying to open the main wardrobe in the room, but it is locked. He kicks it open: it gives.*
He touches the console beside the bed to stop the lights going on and off. The room is semi-dark, the light red. He opens the wardrobe cautiously. As it opens the wardrobe lights up, to reveal an illuminated row of vulgar shoes and boots belonging to a spiv: leopard-skin and crocodile shoes, flashy boots with spurs, cowboy boots, etc.
When he's taken all this in, CLINT *removes his own boots and selects a*

*pair of shoes to wear, like someone choosing a chocolate from a full
box. He tries them but it's a struggle; they're too small, they'll never fit.
He tries walking in them but he falls over, laughing. None of them fit.*

INT./ EXT. BACK OF SQUAT. DAY
CLINT *shouts out of the window to* MUFFDIVER *waiting impatiently
below.*
CLINT: Yo!
MUFFDIVER: What's it like?
CLINT: Round up the posse!
    (MUFFDIVER *is ecstatic. Under his breath, to himself, as a
    celebration, he mutters.*)

EXT. FRONT OF SQUAT. BUILDING. DAY
MUFFDIVER: Round up the fucking posse! Tsa-Tsa!

EXT. STREET. DAY
MUFFDIVER *hurries through the streets, pleased. As he goes, he sees*
BIKE. *Indicates for* BIKE *to go over to him.* BIKE *cycles along beside
him.*
MUFFDIVER: Found us a place to live.
    (BIKE *hits the horn on his bike in acknowledgement.*)

EXT. DINER/STREET. DAY
Outside the diner. SYLVIE *and a middle-aged man, not extravagantly
dressed or posh, have just left the place.* SYLVIE *looks quite smart. She
smiles and talks animatedly.* MUFFDIVER *stops, then follows them.
The man waves at a cab. They both get in.* MUFFDIVER *suddenly
decides to start chasing the cab. It stops at traffic lights.* MUFFDIVER
is looking in the window: the guy has his hand up SYLVIE's *skirt. The
cab moves away.*
SYLVIE *pulls down the window.* MUFFDIVER *runs beside the cab.*
MUFFDIVER: (*Through window*) We've got a place. 14 Whitehall
    Gardens. Top flat. OK.
    (*He smiles at the guy.
    Stay with* SYLVIE *in the cab a few seconds. The guy looks at her.
    She puts her head back and laughs.*)

EXT. DOORWAY/SCAFFOLDING. DAY
BURNS *standing in a doorway, his possessions around him. He's*

always cheerful, despite everything. MUFFDIVER *goes to him.* BURNS *gives him money.* MUFFDIVER *is surprised by the amount.*

MUFFDIVER: How you doing Burns – clubs busy?

BURNS: Long weekend, big demand in the clubs up West. I could easily shift a couple of hundred through the bouncers – I know them all, I got most of them their jobs. Have you got it?

MUFFDIVER: More? Fuck it. I'm really short of supplies right now.

BURNS: By the way, I've had the word. Mr G's ready to see you.

MUFFDIVER: Yeah, I heard. We need him, now.

BURNS: Where shall I tell him to come?

MUFFDIVER: I've found the premises. I've got us a luxury business base.

BURNS: For all of us?

MUFFDIVER: Yeah, you'll have your own room. Burns, your posse needs you. (*Pause.*) How's your stomach?

BURNS: Making noises.

INT. LIVING ROOM OF SQUAT. DAY

Later that day. MUFFDIVER *and* CLINT *have taken possession of the squat and moved their gear in.* CLINT *is wrapped in the leopard-skin carpets and wearing a cowboy hat.*

MUFFDIVER *is pacing, really wound up.*

CLINT: I did good, right, in getting this place? Muff?

MUFFDIVER: Yeah. Didn't I say I'd take care of you? Who needs shoes with these carpets? I have to stop myself –

CLINT: What?

MUFFDIVER: Feeling too happy. In case it don't last. We can really do something here.

CLINT: You mean parties?

MUFFDIVER: I mean as a business base. And I could kiss her here. This is just the venue . . . for a first kiss.

CLINT: Sylvie won't even turn up. And even if she comes she won't stay.

MUFFDIVER: She'll come. (*Pause.*) She's desperate.
(*Now we see the posse walk in through the door one by one, carrying their ragged possessions.* BIKE *comes in apprehensively, with nothing but his bicycle.* BURNS *is a Scotsman, unemployed, fiftyish.* TOM-TOM, *a white Rasta, late thirties, a junkie.*)

BURNS: (*To* CLINT) Home!

CLINT: Yeah!

19

Cut to:

INT. LIVING ROOM OF SQUAT. DAY
They're unpacking their things and admiring the squat. They choose rooms for themselves and lay out their sleeping bags. BURNS *is changing the locks on the door and he chats away to* TOM-TOM *who's laying out his stuff in a corner of the room.*
Then SYLVIE *walks in through the door. She is carrying a trumpet and some other belongings over her shoulder.*
MUFFDIVER: You need a room here Sylvie. Only the best for you.
BURNS: Yeah, only the best.
     (SYLVIE *looks around.*)
MUFFDIVER: We're gonna fix it up and everything, aren't we
     Burns? Furniture. Hot water.
TOM-TOM: Cold water, even.
SYLVIE: Where's little Clint? Has he got his clothes on?
MUFFDIVER: How about a spliff? Bike, roll Sylvie a spliff.
     (BIKE *scuttles off across the squat.*)
TOM-TOM: Give us a toot.
     (*She plays a long sad note on the trumpet.* BURNS *looks at the*

others approvingly. MUFFDIVER *watches her, utterly entranced.*
He's never been in love like this before.
He thinks for a moment then he rushes into Clint's room.)

INT. CLINT'S ROOM. DAY
CLINT, *absorbed in his own world, isn't aware that* SYLVIE's *arrived.*
He's sitting on the bed with two pairs of boots from the wardrobe. He's
trying, with a knife, to cut around the toe so they fit.
MUFFDIVER *shoves him off the bed and then prods the mattress*
energetically, testing it. He also whacks the buttons on the console
beside the bed. The 'effects' go crazy.
MUFFDIVER: This is good. Total theatre, man.
CLINT: Look at these shoes. I'm on my way. Walking.
    (MUFFDIVER *makes a face.*)
    They're for work not for best.
MUFFDIVER: What work? You dealing for someone else?
CLINT: In the diner. They're pretty. Except they don't fit.
    (MUFFDIVER *looks at the room in a businesslike manner. But*
    still finds it difficult to broach the subject on his mind.)
MUFFDIVER: So what exactly is happening here?
CLINT: Oh fucking no. This is exclusively my room.
MUFFDIVER: Yeah, granted. But there's one drawback.
CLINT: There's no drawback.
MUFFDIVER: Listen to me.
CLINT: I climbed the drainpipe!
MUFFDIVER: It's a double room. That interests me.
CLINT: Tsa-Tsa. But does it interest the other person?
MUFFDIVER: Yeah. It does. It interests them.
CLINT: My arse it interests. What other person is it?
    (*We see, but they do not,* SYLVIE *in the room.*)
    There's no other person. I'm the only other person you got.
MUFFDIVER: I love her. I'm addicted to her.
    (*They turn and* SYLVIE *is standing in the doorway.* MUFFDIVER
    is embarrassed, but continues, shyly, gently.)
    How would you like this room?
    (*He pummels the bed histrionically while activating the lights.*
    The TV shoots out of the wall, with the old dinner still intact on
    the panel.)
SYLVIE: My God. Shoe heaven.
CLINT: Yeah, they're only for work, not for best.

21

SYLVIE: Will that man really give you a job?

CLINT: Yeah –

(MUFFDIVER *activates the curtains to distract her.*)

SYLVIE: (*To* CLINT) Clint's settled in here – aren't you, little mouse?

CLINT: (*Sarcastic*) But wouldn't this suit you? Nice duvet, nice mattress, nice MUFFDIVER on top of you –

(SYLVIE *laughs.* MUFFDIVER *is furious, glares at* CLINT *and throws a shoe at him.* SYLVIE *indicates for* MUFFDIVER *to go to her. When he does, she puts her arms around him and kisses him. She indicates to* CLINT *to go to her. She does the same to him. Then she gently pushes the two of them together, encouraging them to hold each other.*)

INT. LIVING ROOM OF SQUAT. DAY

Later that day. BURNS *and* CLINT *together.* CLINT *is getting the practical* BURNS *to cut open the toes of an especially vulgar pair of red cowboy boots covered in metal studs – using a big knife.*

SYLVIE *over the other side of the room practises the trumpet.*

BIKE *is fixing his bicycle.*

TOM-TOM *is asleep on the floor, on his back, music-box beside him. The door to another room is open and* MUFFDIVER *is hurrying about with his possessions, settling in.*

BURNS: (*Working and eating*) You sure this is what you want, Clint boy?

CLINT: Burns, the point is moot. I'm going to wear the boot. (*Pause.*) Ol' Muffdiver is starting to get pretty heavy with people. He wasn't always like that, was he? He was sweet.

BURNS: You knew each other at school, right?

INT. MUFFDIVER'S ROOM. DAY

This room, which he's moving into, is small and virtually empty, except for several tailor's dummies on stands. Slightly eerie.

MUFFDIVER *has put out two sleeping bags, side by side. Now he's adjusting the pillows, etc. He's unpacked his things neatly.*

INT. LIVING ROOM OF SQUAT. DAY

CLINT: (*To* BURNS) There was this day, Burns, man. Me an' Muffdiver stole some LSD from someone at school. And there was another boy who wanted acid badly. So Muff got this stuff and went to him and sold it for a lot of money. I remember, we were in the school cloakroom and he had this money in his hand and his whole face brightened up like I'd never seen it before. He thought he could do anything. I reckon he wanted his whole life to be like that moment.

BURNS: Listen, Clint, these boots . . . Well try 'em on.

(CLINT *puts on the boots, with his bare toes sticking out through the end.*)

CLINT: Great. Thanks Burns, I really appreciate it.

BURNS: Why don't you just buy a cheap pair? Are you sure they're right for restaurant work?

CLINT: Clint is skint.

BURNS: What happens if it rains?

(CLINT *pulls the boots off. There are two plastic bags beside* BURNS, *in which he keeps sandwiches and food.* CLINT *empties the bags neatly, shakes out the crumbs and puts the bags over his feet. He puts on the boots again, and stands there clicking his heels together.*)

CLINT: Olé! Ready for the street.

BURNS: What you gonna sell on the street? Has he given you something?

CLINT: No. I gotta ask him now. Then I'm out sellin' for the last time. Then I'll buy a new pair. The new shoes are due, the shoes –

(*They watch as* MUFFDIVER *calls* SYLVIE.)

MUFFDIVER: Sylvie, Sylvie.

INT. MUFFDIVER'S BEDROOM. DAY

SYLVIE *and* MUFFDIVER. *He is apprehensive . . . but determined. His clothes on one dummy, hers on another.*

SYLVIE: All your little things . . . laid out neat and tidy. (*Pause.*) And my things too.

(MUFFDIVER *opens his hand to show her a bag of smack.*)

SYLVIE: Do you take smack?

MUFFDIVER: (*Slightly amused*) But Clint does, off and on. (*Pretentious.*) I prefer drugs of illusion. (*Pause.*) Kiss. (*He goes to kiss her. She retreats.*) Don't. Just try me out.

23

INT. LIVING ROOM. DAY

Later, in the living room, the whole posse there. CLINT *and* MUFFDIVER *having a serious and loud argument.*

MUFFDIVER: No, man, that's not possible –

CLINT: Please, Muffdiver, give me thirty.

MUFFDIVER: Fucking thirty! (*To the others*) Hey, Tom-Tom, Bike, what's he saying to me? He's saying give him thirty!

CLINT: (*Appealing to the others*) Yeah, that's all. Sylvie.

BURNS: What's the lad want?

TOM-TOM: Thirty Es and As to sell tonight. No chance.

MUFFDIVER: (*To* CLINT) Come on, man, you a jerk off now. I can't take you seriously as a salesman.

CLINT: Thirty ecstasy, thirty acid, and some ME-35. Sale or return. I'm shit-hot reliable. An A-1 salesman, like everyone here. You know what it's for. The footwear it there, in the shop waiting for me.

MUFFDIVER: Yeah, Mr Poet, last time I leaned forward with you, you took half the stuff yourself and gave away the rest.
(MUFFDIVER *starts to look down at* CLINT's *feet, and pulls up his trouser bottoms to reveal the red cowboy boots with the toes in plastic bags sticking out at the end. He invites everyone to look.*)
Hey, hey . . .
(*The others move in closer* SYLVIE *puts her hand in her mouth to stop herself laughing.* BURNS *is annoyed by their mirth. But* CLINT *doesn't lose his dignity.*)

CLINT: Yeah, a good price for me, a good price for you, that's how I get the new shoe.

SYLVIE: (*Appealing*) Muffdiver –

CLINT: You haven't had the childhood I been through. Messages from there are still reaching me. Sexually abused. My father shooting me up with H when I was thirteen –

MUFFDIVER: Exactly my point.

CLINT: What?

MUFFDIVER: You not used to paying for it.

CLINT: Then he got murdered –

BURNS: You gonna get murdered, son. People looking for you with iron bars.

CLINT: Children's homes, probation officers, trials, beatings, shit, shit.

MUFFDIVER: Yeah, Yeah.

CLINT: All I want is some shoes to get my life started!
(BIKE, TOM-TOM *and* MUFFDIVER *laugh*.)

INT. STAIRS/HALLWAY/BOOT ROOM/SUFI CENTRE. DAY
CLINT *and* MUFFDIVER *walk slowly downstairs,* MUFFDIVER *with his arm around him.* CLINT *is looking very down.*
MUFFDIVER: I lose my temper, man. You know me. I'm nervous about Sylvie. I want her so much. When I look at her I can't understand why she isn't mine. (*Pause.*) Here's the stuff you wanted to sell.
(*And he gives him the Es and As.*)
CLINT: I knew you'd come through.
(*Now they stop at the open door of the Sufi Centre. Curious, they wander in.*)
Look, look.
(*A group of people are sitting cross-legged on the floor. A guided meditation is taking place.* DR BUBBA *leads them through it.*)
DR BUBBA: (*To group*) Now you're relaxed, let's concentrate on

breathing. Count your breaths in and out. One, two, three.
Slowly, slowly, from the stomach. You are not, I say not, I
repeat not, blowing up a balloon. This is to slow us down.
This enables us to see our lives clearly for a few minutes.
(*When* CLINT *turns to look at* MUFFDIVER *he sees him leaving.*)

MUFFDIVER: Business.

(CLINT *closes his eyes, takes a breath, smiles to himself relaxedly
and puts the drugs in his pocket. When he does take a squint he
sees a row of shoes. This is deeply pleasing to him.*

*He chooses an excellent pair of shoes and, removing the cowboy
boots, tries them on. They fit. Bliss.*

*He is creeping out of the door in his new shoes, blowing kisses at
them, when* DR BUBBA *is behind him.*)

DR BUBBA: You are in love with those shoes?

(CLINT *continues walking away.*)

Do they fit?

(CLINT *finally stops and turns to face* DR BUBBA.)

I am your neighbour, Dr Bubba. This morning, why didn't
you come in through the front door? (*Pause.*) Let's see. Are
they not a little floppy, my boy? You need a size less, I
imagine. Lift up. Lift up, if you please.

(DR BUBBA *removes* CLINT'S *new trainers from his feet.*)

Now, let's look here. (*At the row of shoes.*) Mr Runcipher –
asleep over there –

(*We see Mr Runcipher swaying and sleeping instead of
meditating.*)

– has a smaller foot and kinder nature. You poor boy.

(*But* CLINT *hurriedly puts the cowboy boots back on, minus
plastic bags.*)

CLINT: No, no, it's OK, thanks a lot, don't worry –

(*A shot of* DR BUBBA'S *sandal next to* CLINT'S *foot.*)

DR BUBBA: But look, my foot and yours are entirely equal.
Clearly you favour the exposed toe. Latest fashion? May I
give you my sandal?

CLINT: Do you have strange powers, Dr Bubba?

DR BUBBA: If I had strange powers, what would you want me to
do for you?

EXT. STREET. DAY

CLINT *in the street, swallowing pills. He stands and watches people as they walk by, looking for potential customers, nodding and hissing at potential buyers. He's determined and singleminded.*

We see BIKE *down the street from him, looking out checking the area, occasionally signalling to* CLINT.

CLINT: Hash? E? A? I got some great E! What do you say? E? A?

Cut to:

EXT. STREET. day

CLINT *in a doorway, taking money from a middle-class white girl and giving her the stuff.*

BIKE *is in the background.*

INT. LIFT. DAY

CLINT *in the lift of a filthy West London Tower block. Two dirty fifteen-year-olds, one white, one black, are in the lift with him. The* WHITE KID *has a cut-up face: chains of stitches.*

WHITE KID: Show us the gear, Mr Eastwood.

CLINT: (*Distracted*) Show us the money.

    (*The black kid pulls out a knife.* CLINT, *now quite stoned, looks at them and laughs. They look down at his feet and start to laugh.*)

EXT. STREET NR HI-TECH BAR. DAY
A couple of TOURISTS, *a German man and woman, with rucksacks, are wandering distractedly in the street. The street* DEALERS, *one by one, spot them, and practically sprint towards them.*
DEALER ONE: Germans . . .
DEALER TWO: Tourists . . .
DEALER THREE: Free money man.
(CLINT *shoves them aside.*)
CLINT: They're my beauties.
Cut to:

EXT. STREET NR HI-TECH BAR. DAY
CLINT *with the* TOURISTS. *They're fascinated by his spiel . . . and his hands all over them, cajoling, wheedling, charming.*
CLINT: (*Picking up a rucksack*) And if you're looking for a cheap hotel . . . and you say you are. How much are you paying? (*Amazed.*) You're being destroyed. Your little Aryan faces are being ripped off. Let me help you. We're all young people.
TOURIST WOMAN: Are you a hotelier?
CLINT: Yes, yes I am. Eastwood House, a hostel for young people in need. This place will cool you.
TOURIST MAN: But there is heating, Mr Eastwood?
CLINT: Underfloor heating, yeah. Overfloor heating. Everything you could want.

EXT. STREET NEAR DINER. DAY
CLINT *with a* BUYER, *a young suited man on the street, near the diner. They talk urgently and quickly. This is* CLINT *in his selling routine. He is professional and convincing, good at this, having done it many times before. He spots the* BUYER *on the street, eye contact: then he goes to him, leading him into a doorway or sidestreet. He really knows how to hustle without frightening the guy.*
CLINT: Yeah, what d'you want? Hash? No. E? Tabs? E, yeah? I've got some good E, burgers not capsules. The purest form. This stuff will chill you, man. Just tip it on your tongue. Taste the fizz. Yeah?
BUYER: How much?
CLINT: Twenty. These are going quickly. How many? Ten? I can do a reduced price for ten. Yeah, going for that?
BUYER: Three.

CLINT: Yeah, little rave? You'll buzz on these. They're the best on the street. Just gimme the money, that's sixty, and you hang right there.
BUYER: Where you going?
CLINT: Five minutes. Two and a half. I can't carry the stuff round with me at great personal risk. Would you?
    (*The* BUYER *is reluctant.* CLINT *hardens.*)
CLINT: You've seen me about. I'm on this corner every night. If you're not satisfied I'll refund your money.
    (*The* BUYER *gives him the money.* CLINT *backs away, and then splits quickly.*)

EXT. STREET OUTSIDE DINER. DAY
Minutes later. CLINT *has walked round to the diner. He watches the waiters keenly. He's also looking for* HEMINGWAY.
Finally he spots him, talking to the barman who's making a line of gloriously coloured cocktails. CLINT *raised his arm in extravagant greeting.* HEMINGWAY *waves at him and nods gravely.* CLINT *points down at his feet, indicating that the present shoes are shit but that the future is promising.*
He looks at MELANIE *and she smiles at him.*
Outside diner a man walks up by CLINT'*s side. It's the* BUYER. *His eyes travel to the* BUYER'*s angry face.* CLINT *is very agitated.*
BUYER: (*Sneering*) Where's my cool E – to chill me, chill me?
    (CLINT *gives it to him.*)

EXT./INT. HI-TECH BAR. DAY
CLINT *enters bar counting his money in the revolving doorway of a seedy hi-tech bar in the area. A notice saying:* NO DRUGS IN THIS ESTABLISHMENT. *Open dealing going on. A guy under the notice, carving up a lump of hash on the table.*
An old black man stands and sings drunkenly, accompanied by someone in the corner on keyboard.
Big dealers in dark glasses sit around with their women.
A cluster of rent boys, some in make-up, twittering around. A couple of women prostitutes, junkies with them. A handful of transvestites, all arguing and chattering.
CLINT *speaks to several people as he walks through to the bar.*
CLINT: Wanting? Wanting? Wanting?
RENT BOY: Not from you, dear.

Cut to:

INT. HI-TECH BAR. DAY
CLINT *is clutching drinks, crisps and cigarettes which he puts down.*
TOM-TOM, SYLVIE *and* FAULKNER *are sitting at the table.*
TOM-TOM: (*Pleased with the drinks*) Hey, this is good.
CLINT: Yeah, why not?
SYLVIE: (*Kissing him*) Generous.
CLINT: What's that on your cheek? (*He looks at her.*) It's OK, I
  thought you were developing a second nose. Hi Faulkner.
  (FAULKNER *insists on kissing him.*)
  (*To them all*) I tell you, I had a good day at the office, I mean
  it. I can be a sweet dealer when I put my mind to it.
SYLVIE: We did good too. Shopping for the squat.
TOM-TOM: And not an item paid for.
  (TOM-TOM *has a new suitcase beside him which he opens. The
  four of them pull out telephones, teapots, ornaments, cutlery,
  lamps, etc. As they look through it* SYLVIE *sees* CLINT *scratching
  his face and pulls his hand down.*)
FAULKNER: Oh yuk, yuk.
CLINT: I'm on fire. I wanna tear my arms off and smash them on
  the table.
SYLVIE: How come?
CLINT: I'm kicking.
SYLVIE: Can't they take you into the rehab?
CLINT: They already threw me out.
SYLVIE: For what?
CLINT: Drug-taking.
  (*They laugh.* SYLVIE *pulls a sporty cap with ear-flaps and an
  adjustable peak out of the suitcase and gives it to* CLINT.)
SYLVIE: Here.
FAULKNER: Oh yeah.
CLINT: Is this really for me then?
  (*She and* FAULKNER *help him put it on – a big procedure,
  accompanied by posing and clapping and laughter.
  From across the bar* CLINT *is watched by a middle-aged black
  guy.*)
SYLVIE: Thought it would suit you.
FAULKNER: Not quite. Put yourself in my hands.
  (FAULKNER *readjusts the cap.*)

Better.

SYLVIE: Isn't he a sweetie?

TOM-TOM: Not bad for a derelict, for a disaster.

(*Among friends,* CLINT *sits back like a rent boy and puts his feet on the table, forgetting the state, of his boots, which people notice. Goes into a stoned reverie.*)

FAULKNER: Clint's so good-looking, apart from the feet and the skin disease. Oh find me a man, someone. Had one today?

CLINT: We're looking after her now.

FAULKNER: Christ. The thing is, Sylvie, people don't realize what hard work it is sucking cock for a living. What a skill and trade it is, like bricklaying. The public think, oh five minutes jaw work and there you are, tax-free millions. But it's dirty, risky and exhausting, your little head bobbing up and down for hours on end. Followed by a mouthful of snot.

CLINT: I don't wanna hear about it. I'm getting a proper job.

FAULKNER: (*Laughs*) It's only prostitution by other means.

CLINT: (*Quietly, to* SYLVIE) Can I see you?

SYLVIE: You're seeing me now.

CLINT: We should do something cultural together. (*Pause.*) You always liked me.

SYLVIE: I do, I do.

CLINT: You won't stay with Muffdiver. He doesn't know that yet. You've made him fall in love with you. It's not a feeling he's accustomed to. Then you'll let him down.

(*She looks at him, surprised by his cruelty.*)

SYLVIE: Stop it.

CLINT: What d'you want, Sylvie?

SYLVIE: What you got? (*Pause.*) You've got to stick with him. He's the only one who knows what's going on.

(*The black guy taps* CLINT *on the shoulder.* CLINT *turns. The guy indicates another black guy, who gets up and takes* CLINT *out into the street.* CLINT *turns to look at* SYLVIE *as he goes.* SYLVIE *and* TOM-TOM *start to pack up their things.*)

Mr G. Tonight?

TOM-TOM: (*To* SYLVIE) Yeah, we better get on with it. You didn't tell Clint?

(*She shakes her head.*)

You tell that boy something and it goes no further than Europe.

EXT. STREET/ELECTRIC CINEMA. DUSK
A BLACK GIRL, *early twenties, a nanny, takes* CLINT *by the arm and leads him through the streets, throwing away his new cap in disgust. Past the Electric Cinema, a few people outside. The* GIRL *walks briskly, and* CLINT *tries to keep up with her.*
CLINT: Headley want to see me? She in a good mood? What's on at the pictures?
GIRL: *La Dolce Vita.*
CLINT: What's that?
    (*The* GIRL *gives him a contemptuous look.*)

INT. HEADLEY'S FLAT. EVENING
Weird music. The atmosphere a mixture of hi-tech late 1980s and hippy eclectic. Indian and African things. Much third-worldism. We are in the living room. Three LITERARY TYPES *talking, a man and two young women, laughing, drinking, all expensively dressed. Various snacks on the table. Beer, wine, champagne.*
CLINT *breaks away from the* GIRL *and takes some salmon from the table.*
LITERARY MAN: And are you a writer too?
CLINT: Yeah. I'm putting down my story. It's pretty sickening, you know. (*To* GIRL.) Tell Headley I'll wait here for her. (*To* LITERARY MAN.) Wanna deal with something real for a change?
GIRL: You come on.
    (*And she pulls* CLINT *away.*)

INT. HEADLEY'S STUDY. EVENING
HEADLEY *is a tall, strong, imposing professor and writer. She is not the type to listen much to others. Her mood can swing from the hard to the sentimental pretty quickly.*
Anyhow, for the time being she ignores CLINT, *who tiptoes around, nervous of her and not wanting to be there at all.*
HEADLEY *is, at the moment, with a woman and baby.* HEADLEY *is pulling clothes out of a cupboard for both child and mother.* HEADLEY *talks continuously.*
HEADLEY: Why do I have to help them? Doesn't the fucking state do anything? I'm not a fucking doctor am I?
    (*She stares straight at* CLINT, *who recoils and turns away moodily.*)

I'm just strong and rich, that's all. So these people come to me every day because they know I'm too guilty and weak to refuse them.

(*She talks to the baby in good Spanish, then gives the woman a gorgeous string of beads, pressing them on the unresisting woman.*)

They're Indian, from Mexico. Sell them if you like.

(*The woman goes, backwards.* HEADLEY *looks at her with contempt, then sits with her head in her hands.*)

CLINT: (*After a pause.*) Headley, I'm here.

HEADLEY: I know, dear, I can hear you scratching.

(*Put out,* CLINT *goes to the birdcage and prods the bird.*)

CLINT: How are you, parrot-face? Want some bush to get outta your face?

(*He fishes some bush out of his bag and gives it to the bird.*)

HEADLEY: It's a toucan. Cyrano. I require that bush, Clint. I intend to get very high.

CLINT: (*Approaching her*) Headley, man, this stuff is fucking steep.

HEADLEY: (*Noticing his boots*) Don't stamp dog-shit into my Persian rug.

CLINT: You haven't got a better pair of shoes by any chance? You know, lying around. They're dear. Doesn't matter if they're only brogues.

HEADLEY: Buy some. You street dealers earn more than I do. Or does that other boy, the rough one, Bill Sykes, control you?

(*She looks at him. He's not answering these kind of questions. He goes round the rug and puts the bush on the table. She makes a note on a piece of paper.*)

CLINT: What you writing? About F. Scott Fitzgerald's books?

HEADLEY: Something about the representation of black women in film. Women noir?

CLINT: Yeah? Oh Headley, you really know how to enjoy yourself.

(HEADLEY *slaps her knee as if summoning a dog or a baby.*
CLINT *starts to get even more nervous.*)

No, Headley, I better get going, you know. I've gotta get some shoes lined up for my job.

HEADLEY: You want to eat, don't you? Here.

(*And she pulls him towards her.*)

Cut to:

33

INT. HEADLEY'S STUDY. EVENING

CLINT *is sitting on* HEADLEY's *knee. She touches his face, hair, hands, partly out of affection, partly out of disinterested love, and partly it is medical examination. Then she cuddles him, saying:*

HEADLEY: 'Thus is his cheek the map of days outworn
   When Beauty lived and died as flowers do now.'
   (CLINT *stares into the distance.*)

Cut to:

INT. HEADLEY'S LIVING ROOM. NIGHT

A little later. The living room of Headley's flat. It is darker now. The three LITERARY TYPES *are present, eating, drinking and laughing, prior to going out for the evening.*

CLINT *is sitting across the room with a plate of food on his knee, eating eagerly.*

One of the LITERARY TYPES *has removed her high heels and waves them at* CLINT *as he eats. He glances up at her and then continues to eat, ignoring this shit.*

LITERARY WOMAN: Let him wear my shoes, they'll suit him.
   (HEADLEY *walks up and down, mainly addressing* CLINT.)

LITERARY MAN: Don't go on, Headley.

HEADLEY: There are crimes that people commit against others. Of course. But there are, to me, more intriguing crimes, the ones that people commit against themselves. These puzzles me, especially as I get older and wish to live to a hundred and fifty. What do I love? This? (*She indicates the room.*) My garden.
   (*The* LITERARY MAN *has filled the* LITERARY WOMAN's *shoe with champagne and now drinks from it.*
   HEADLEY *hits a button on the CD. We hear Allegri's* Miserere Mei.)
   Jugged hare. The Beatles. But what could you say, Clint? What do you love? Drugs.
   (*And she laughs scornfully.* CLINT *is, by now, bent over, dinner on his lap, half off the chair. He looks up at her. She drags thoughtfully on her joint.*)
   No one need make you bleed. You'll do it to yourself.
   (CLINT *is angry with her. But he can't speak. He puts his food down, and falls over on to his knees, crawls a bit, and finally walks and runs out.*)

EXT. STREET NR DINER. NIGHT
The music continues. CLINT *has left* HEADLEY'S *place. Now he relaxes and perks up as he walks past the diner. Two waitresses are outside, including* MELANIE. *He's about to strike up conversation with her when he spots* HEMINGWAY.
Cut to:

EXT. DINER. NIGHT
MELANIE *watches* CLINT *go. He steps into a puddle, soaking the exposed toe.*
Cut to:

EXT. STREET NEAR OFF-LICENCE. NIGHT
Further up the street CLINT *sees* BURNS *coming out of an off-licence carrying bottles of beer.*
He walks on. Further up he sees BIKE *on his bicycle, riding without hands, carrying booze and food. He cycles past* CLINT, *not noticing him. Maybe this is an hallucination and* CLINT *accepts it equably.*

INT. SQUAT. NIGHT
CLINT *enters the flat and sees there's no one in. He wanders around until he sees the* TOURISTS *sitting leaning against their rucksacks, with a picnic spread out in front of them.*
CLINT: So you got in all right?
TOURIST WOMAN: Which is our room?
CLINT: Err . . . this way.
    (CLINT *leads them upstairs into Burns's room, which is, naturally, full of his stuff. There are photographs of his children, his handyman's gear, clothes, etc.*)
    The rent, s'il vous plaît.
TOURIST WOMAN: Now, Mr Eastwood?
CLINT: Yeah, on the button and no travellers' cheques accepted.
TOURIST MAN: But this is someone else's room.
CLINT: This? (*He shoves some of Burns's gear aside.*) Burns is moving out tonight. Make yourself comfortable. I'm just going to have a sleep, then I'm going out to buy some shoes, for work, not for best.
    (*The* TOURIST MAN *counts out the money.*)

INT. SQUAT. MUFFDIVER'S ROOM. NIGHT
CLINT *goes into Muffdiver's room – sees Muffdiver's and Sylvie's stuff side by side, which surprises and hurts him. He goes through Muffdiver's things, finding nothing of interest but a knife.*
He gropes through Sylvie's things and finds three pairs of old ballet shoes that would have fitted a child, a kid and a teenager. He puts them back.
Also amongst her things he finds a number of literary paperbacks: Jean Rhys, Willa Cather, Jane Bowles, Jayne Anne Phillips. Plus several full notebooks of her own writing. He flicks through the pages, which are densely written.
At the door, on his way out, he has a brainwave. He goes to the dummies and puts his hand up inside one of them. He takes most of Muffdiver's stash of money, leaving a few quid behind, out of generosity. He is very pleased with this.

EXT. ROOF OF SQUAT. NIGHT
CLINT *puts most of the money under a brick on the roof, taking a little for himself.*

INT. CLINT'S BEDROOM. NIGHT
A couple of hours later. CLINT *has crashed out on his bed, eyes open, staring at the ceiling. The curtains move slowly back and forth, billowing in the wind. He hears noises from outside: chanting from the Sufi Centre below mixed with noises from the living room in a hallucinogenic blend. He gets up.*

INT. LIVING ROOM OF SQUAT. NIGHT
CLINT *opens the door on to an odd scene. A hallucination, the only time in this film. And only for a few seconds.*
He sees SYLVIE *wearing a ballerina's tutu and dancing.* BURNS *is dressed as Father Christmas.* BIKE, *in a yellow jersey and cycling shorts, is suspended from the ceiling on his bicycle with a tray of cocaine across the handlebars.*
TOM-TOM *is playing the guitar dressed as Keith Richards.*
There is music. The entire scene seems to be taking place in a snowstorm.
CLINT *blinks several times and the scene returns to normal. Even then it is a pretty odd scene.*
BIKE, BURNS *and* TOM-TOM *are frantically fixing the place up.*

BURNS *is installing the twee table lamps which* SYLVIE *and* TOM-
TOM *stole that afternoon.* (*Obviously, in the room, until now, there is
only an overhead light or some other arrangement.*)
SYLVIE *is preparing drinks for later.*
TOM-TOM *is arranging crisps.*
BIKE *is washing up.*
SYLVIE: Were you there all the time?
   (TOM-TOM *hands him a dishcloth and a pile of plates.*)
TOM-TOM: Get wiping, man.
CLINT: Wipe your own arse.
SYLVIE: Mr G's coming to see Muffdiver.
CLINT: What for?
TOM-TOM: (*Indicating plates*) I thought you were interested in
   restaurant work.
   (CLINT *gives him a dirty look.* TOM-TOM *regards him
   resentfully.*)
SYLVIE: (*Going to the trouble to explain*) Mr G's the top man, you
   know that. Sign on with him and you don't have any drug-
   flow problems.
   (CLINT *wipes the plates, making sure* TOM-TOM *sees him.*)
SYLVIE: (*To* CLINT) Muff's gonna do a big buy. Keep us all going
   for weeks.
CLINT: Which we gotta sell on the street.
SYLVIE: Yeah, it's work for all of us.
   (*Making sure* TOM-TOM *is watching,* CLINT *throws one of the
   plates in the air and catches it on the end of his finger and twirls it
   around dramatically and impressively, nodding at* TOM-TOM.
   Now MUFFDIVER *hurries into the room in businesslike mood. He
   takes everything in quickly. Everyone working away
   satisfactorily, except* CLINT, *with a plate whirling on his finger.*)
MUFFDIVER: Great. Good, everyone. (*Snaps finger at* CLINT.)
   You. (*To her*) Sylvie. Boardroom.
   (*He jabs at* BIKE. BIKE *looks at him eagerly, ready to respond.*
   MUFFDIVER *nods.* BIKE *obviously knows what to do.*)

INT. LANDING. NIGHT
BIKE *gets a pot of tea for three set out on a tray from dumb waiter and
goes into Clint's room.*

INT. CLINT'S ROOM. NIGHT

MUFFDIVER, SYLVIE *and* CLINT *in the room.* CLINT *moves in and out of consciousness, resentful, confused.* MUFFDIVER *excited. He chops out a line of coke for himself.*

MUFFDIVER: This is an executive meeting – of the top executives of Muffdiver, Sylvie and Clint Eastwood Limited, PLC.

SYLVIE: What's PLC?

MUFFDIVER: Posse Limited Company.

(BIKE, *like a servant, is handing out the tea.* CLINT *tries to talk.*)

MUFFDIVER: You wanna speak? Right. Bike.

(BIKE *takes out a notebook and pencil. Meanwhile* MUFFDIVER *snorts up the coke, looks up and listens.*)

CLINT: You always in charge of everything.

MUFFDIVER: Yeah, I got the initiative. But it's the three of us – three business partners – doing this shit together.

CLINT: Doing what, though? What? What? What?

MUFFDIVER: Tonight, it's tonight, we're going big. This posse can deal E, A, M-25, M-26 – to the whole district. We got the contacts, the premises, the staff. The market's expanding, you know it is. Supply and demand, those cats out there can't get high enough. Course, there can't be any weak links. Weak links have to be taken care of. (*He stares at* CLINT.)

SYLVIE: Sounds good.

MUFFDIVER: Yeah? Say yeah.

CLINT: You can't boss Clint around. It don't suit me. Gotta go my own way.

SYLVIE: (*Gently to* CLINT) Let's give it a chance. Let's get somewhere, all of us. Think of all the shoes you'll be able to buy. In two years you can buy your own shoe shop.

MUFFDIVER: Right. Mr G'll be here in a minute. Let's make a good impression. Meeting's adjourned.

INT. LIVING ROOM. NIGHT

MUFFDIVER *is inspecting the posse in a line-up.*

MUFFDIVER: Bike, don't slow things down. Burns, how's the special cool lighting going?

BURNS: It's on.

(*He touches a crumb off* BURNS's *face. He inspects* CLINT's *shoes, etc.*)

MUFFDIVER: Right. Tom-Tom, you used to be a Master chef . . .
     If they want drinks . . . Got any ice? (*Panicking.*) Mr G's only
     used to the best.
     (*The lights have already flickered during the line-up. Then the
     lights go completely.*)
     Burns, fix the fucking lights, man!

EXT. FRONT OF SQUAT BUILDING. NIGHT
Now we see MR G *and his posse getting out of their car, walking up to
the house.*

INT. LIVING ROOM OF SQUAT. NIGHT
The lights BURNS *has fixed up, chintzy little things, are flicking on
and off.*
Cheering.
BURNS *tries to fix the lights.*
The front door bell rings in the living room.
The two German TOURISTS *walk in.*
TOURIST WOMAN: Mr Eastwood –
TOURIST MAN: Mr Eastwood, the lights in our room are
     extinguishing onwards and offwards.
TOM-TOM: What room?
TOURIST MAN: Mr Eastwood has rented us a room upstairs. He
     said we could chill out. It's cool.
     (BURNS *looks at* CLINT.)
BURNS: Yeah?
     (MUFFDIVER *is confused. He goes to the German* TOURIST
     MAN *and holds out his hand.*)
MUFFDIVER: Mr G?
TOURIST MAN: Mr Wolf. Please to meet you.

INT. HALL OF HOUSE. NIGHT
MR G *and his posse have come up the hallway and are now by the
Sufi Centre.* MR G *and the others look suspiciously into the Sufi
Centre.*

INT. LIVING ROOM OF SQUAT. NIGHT
(*Same time.*)
MUFFDIVER: Who are these people?
TOURIST MAN: Mr Eastwood, the landlord here –

BURNS: Mr Eastwood the landlord? (*To them.*) You sleeping in
my room?
TOURIST WOMAN: It was rented to us. How do you say it? All in?
(TOM-TOM and SYLVIE *restrain* BURNS *as he struggles to get*
CLINT.)
TOM-TOM: All in what?

INT. SUFI CENTRE. NIGHT
Meanwhile, downstairs, DR BUBBA *rises and goes forward to greet*
MR G, *who has a smart young black* ASSISTANT *with him and two
young women, one black, one white.*
DR BUBBA: Please, you are all welcome. Remove your shoes.
(MUFFDIVER *rushes downstairs into the Sufi Centre, behind* MR
G, *and sees the indignity he is about to suffer.*
Meanwhile the German TOURISTS *are coming down the stairs,
turning to the group.*)
TOURISTS: I tell you nothing for something, don't stay in this
place.
(MUFFDIVER *is virtually bent over double, so grovelling is he.*
MR G *turns and sees him.*

40

MUFFDIVER *gestures him and his posse out of the place, tripping over meditators as he goes.*)
MUFFDIVER: Mr G, you can't choose your neighbours, can you? Come upstairs for some refreshments. Sorry. Sorry.

INT. LIVING ROOM OF SQUAT. NIGHT
MUFFDIVER *leads* MR G *and his posse into the room.*
MUFFDIVER *brings them in and they stand there waiting for* MR G *to sit down. The girls talk to each other.*
Then the black woman goes to BIKE'*s bicycle and takes it.*
TOM-TOM: Mr G, Mrs G, hallo.
MUFFDIVER: Welcome, Welcome.
    (TOM-TOM *nods at* BIKE. *The woman climbs on to the bike and honks the horn.* MR G *grins for the first time. We can see that* BIKE *is becoming very anxious and is about to react.*
    MUFFDIVER *glares at him.*
    BURNS *is still furious with* CLINT *about the* TOURISTS *and surreptitiously tries to whack him.*
    MUFFDIVER *glares at* BURNS.)
MUFFDIVER: Burns!
    (MR G *finally sits down. His posse sit down, the black girl on Bike's bike.*
    SYLVIE *offers them all peanuts.*)
Cut to:

INT. SQUAT LIVING ROOM. NIGHT
MUFFDIVER – *and this is one of his specialities – is doing conjuring tricks for* MR G. *He wears a cape and top-hat. Behind,* SYLVIE, *who has dressed up rather pathetically, plays the trumpet.*
MUFFDIVER *pulls balls out of his mouth, strings of handkerchiefs out of the white girl's ear, etc.*
MUFFDIVER: Is it real or is it false? No one wants too much reality, we all know that.
    (MR G *has been looking around at the place with much curiosity.*)
MR G: When have I been here before?
ASSISTANT: It's Jimmy's place.
CLINT: He's lending it to us.
ASSISTANT: Really?
    (*To end the act* MR G *nods at* MUFFDIVER. *It's over.*
    MUFFDIVER *bows.*

41

MUFFDIVER *indicates to* TOM-TOM. TOM-TOM *takes charge*.)

TOM-TOM: This way, please, if you don't mind. Just for a few minutes, to ensure privacy. Let's go through, I mean up.

INT. SQUAT LANDING. NIGHT

Everyone filing out of the squat. CLINT *moaning and cursing as they go,* BIKE *protectively carrying his bicycle.*

BURNS: (*German accent*) A word, Mr Eastwood the landlord.

INT. LIVING ROOM OF SQUAT. NIGHT

MR G *and his* ASSISTANT *and* MUFFDIVER *sit in serious conference, drinking. The* ASSISTANT *has his briefcase open, listening to* MUFFDIVER *as he puts his proposal.*

EXT. ROOF. NIGHT

The others, including MR G's *girls, are on the roof of the squat.* BIKE *sits looking through the bars of his bicycle at everyone, especially* CLINT, *who he's happy to see with* SYLVIE.

CLINT *takes* SYLVIE's *hand and leads her to the edge of the roof. His hand is over the brick (where he concealed the money) as he talks.*

CLINT: I made some money today. I wanted to give you some.

SYLVIE: Oh no. What about your shoes?

CLINT: I'll take care of that tomorrow. And I start work the next day. I'm pretty confident about things, Sylvie.

SYLVIE: (*Takes the money*) Thanks, Clint. Thanks.

CLINT: Top of the world. I need to get out of London. Let's go . . . Let's go to the countryside tomorrow, yeah? I know a good place where there's not too many farmers. What d'you say?

(*She nods at him.*)

INT. SQUAT LIVING ROOM. NIGHT

MUFFDIVER *and* MR G *and his* ASSISTANT *in heavy conference.*

ASSISTANT: Everything seems agreed then. Give us the upfront investment now, as arranged. The delivery of everything you've ordered will be in two days.

MUFFDIVER: (Excited) And, Mr G, both of you, I tell you, I've got the best on-the-street salesmen in the area. My people are hand-trained. Dealing's no longer for amateurs. I want to get a smooth home-delivery service started. Like in Chicago –

'The publisher with the strongest film list is Faber.' *Guardian*

Whether you are an avid film buff or an occasional cinema-goer, Faber's books on film studies, biographies and screenplays are sure to be of interest.

If you would like further information about Faber's film list, please fill in your name and address and return this card to Faber and Faber. (Do not affix postage stamps if posted in the United Kingdom, Channel Islands or Isle of Man)

Name_____

Address_____

_____

Postcode_____

Promotions Dept
Faber and Faber Ltd
3 Queen Square
LONDON
WC1N 3BR

'Hash-to-go', 'Call-a-snort', 'Dial-a-spliff'. Bikes, mopeds, a courier service.

ASSISTANT: Hand-trained, you say.

MUFFDIVER: Yeah. (*Loses confidence.*) Yeah.

MR G: Hand-trained by whom?

MUFFDIVER: By me, Mr G.

(MR G *and his* ASSISTANT *look at each other.* MUFFDIVER *gets up.*)

INT. MUFFDIVER'S BEDROOM. NIGHT
We see MUFFDIVER's *confident, smug face as he walks towards the tailor's dummy in the bedroom.*

EXT. ROOF. NIGHT
The others on the roof. We see CLINT's *face, eyes closed, breathing deeply, looking up at the sky.* BURNS *eating a huge sandwich.* TOM-TOM *sitting there, talking to the girls.*

INT. MUFFDIVER'S ROOM. NIGHT
We see MUFFDIVER's *hand reaching into the back of the dummy. We see him pulling some money out. Counts it; realizes it's not all there; gets agitated; counts it again; searches again. Searches the room for money. Finally gives up. Is furious.*

INT. STAIRS OF SQUAT. NIGHT
MUFFDIVER *tells* MR G *that the money has gone and he can't pay him.* MUFFDIVER *is speechless. The sad and comic sight of him telling them the money's gone and them rising in irritation to leave.*
The others come back into the room, the women going out with MR G.
MR G'S ASSISTANT *just turns and points at* MUFFDIVER.

INT. STAIRS OF SQUAT. NIGHT
Rest of troup stand watching MR G. *leaving. We reverse on to* MUFFDIVER's *face as everyone is filing past him.*

INT. LIVING ROOM OF SQUAT. NIGHT
MR G *and his posse have gone.* MUFFDIVER *is running around the room, screaming, attempting to smash everything, as they try to stop him.* BURNS *keeps grabbing at him. The others are hunting around, under chairs, carpets, etc., for the purloined money.* CLINT *searches*

43

especially hard.

MUFFDIVER: Where's my fucking money, you fucking bastards, where is it, who's got it? I'll kill you for humiliating me! Mr G thinks I'm a total jerk-off and idiot fool prick total arsehole, Jesus! Search, search, you useless bastards! Who's got it?

(*He grabs* BURNS *by the throat, pulling a knife on him.*)

MUFFDIVER: You desperate old man, it must be you!

CLINT: Muffdiver, man –

(*He turns on* CLINT.)

MUFFDIVER: So it was you!

TOM-TOM: Bike's brother was in here too at one point.

SYLVIE: And the tourists.

BURNS: (*German accent, laughing*) Yes it was them. Mr Eastwood the landlord.

(MUFFDIVER *sinks down in despair. The posse look at each other, some laughing.* SYLVIE *goes to him, reaching down and touching him.* CLINT *watches her. She looks up at him.*)

CLINT: Tomorrow, yeah? You an' me.

MUFFDIVER'S BEDROOM. NIGHT

MUFFDIVER *stands naked at the window of his room, trying to fix old sheets or dirty curtains to the window frame. He's banging away with hammer and nails and keeps hitting his thumb. The wind and rain blow through the window.*

When he's done this he sits in bed. He counts the money he still has and counts the tabs and capsules and 'burgers' he has in his possession.

We then see that SYLVIE *is there in the room with him. With great dignity she has put her things out on a packing case. She cleans her face with cotton wool. She moisturizes her face with care and combs her hair.*

MUFFDIVER *looks at his drugs and money and then at her. At first he doesn't catch her eye. They then look at each other. Apprehension on his face.*

She goes to him.

From outside, through this scene, we hear the others playing rhythmically on cans and trumpet and other homemade instruments. It's a loud, hypnotic sound, getting faster and faster.

INT. LIVING ROOM OF SQUAT. NIGHT
*The men – CLINT, BURNS, TOM-TOM – on the floor in the living
room. BIKE sitting beside his bicycle.*
*The door to Muffdiver's room is ajar. Human noises are heard. CLINT
glances nervously at the door. He has Sylvie's trumpet at his lips,
giving it a toot now and again.*
*BURNS watches CLINT and sees how disappointed and yet hopeful he
is.*
TOM-TOM: (*To* BURNS) What's your real trade then?
BURNS: Electrician, me. This line of work isn't something I
    thought I'd get into when I was young, bodyguarding
    someone called Muffdiver, walking round with LSD
    strapped to me scrotum. Eh Bike?
    (BIKE *opens his mouth to speak but some inner grief prevents him.
    They all look at him in anticipation but nothing comes.*
    CLINT *toots on the trumpet,* BURNS *taps an empty Coke tin with
    a pencil,* TOM-TOM *drums on his knees. They grin at each other.*)

INT. SQUAT. MORNING
Next morning. CLINT *has got up early. He's finished making
sandwiches. He pops a couple of tomatoes into a bag.* TOM-TOM *is
asleep on the floor.* BIKE *also asleep, next to his bicycle.*
To his surprise CLINT *also sees* FAULKNER *asleep on the floor,
covered in other people's clothes, a pair of high heels beside him, a
dress flung over a chair.*
FAULKNER: Going somewhere?
CLINT: Tsa-Tsa – bit of fresh country air up our nostrils.
FAULKNER: All of you?
CLINT: No way.
Cut to:

INT. SQUAT LIVING ROOM. DAY
The others are stirring now. CLINT *squats down and waits at the far
side of the room.* BIKE *and* TOM-TOM *are moving about.*
Finally, MUFFDIVER *emerges from his room, in leopard-skin print
bathrobe, looks around, greets his posse, kisses* FAULKNER's *hand and
goes to* CLINT.)
MUFFDIVER: Sleep all right?
    (CLINT *nods.*)
    Tsa-Tsa, you look good anyway. Combed your hair too.

45

(*He grabs* CLINT's *sandwich bag, looks inside and pulls out a mouldy-looking tomato.*)
What's this?
(*He notices* CLINT *is holding a rolled-up towel.*)
Going to the seaside?
(CLINT *Shrugs.*)
Was it you? Tell me.

CLINT: No, man.

MUFFDIVER: Don't go anywhere today, I wanna talk about my night with Sylvie. It was the best night I ever had – ever. Don't be like that. Clint, I still like talking to you.
(*Not getting any response,* MUFFDIVER *goes off.*)

INT. MUFFDIVER'S BEDROOM. DAY
CLINT *slowly opens the door to Muffdiver's bedroom.* SYLVIE *is lying in bed, facing away from him. He holds his sandwich bag.*

SYLVIE: There are some days when you just know you're never gonna get up.
(CLINT *squatting behind her, strokes her shoulders, neck and face.*)

CLINT: We still on?

SYLVIE: What? Oh, it's you.

CLINT: For the outing. You said.

SYLVIE: What?
(*They look at each other. Now* MUFFDIVER *is behind them.*)

MUFFDIVER: What's he doing?((*To* CLINT.) What you want in here?

CLINT: I'm calling a board meeting.

MUFFDIVER: You're up to something. The shoe is through.
(MUFFDIVER *starts to throw him out. They fight.*)

CLINT: Fuck you!

SYLVIE: Stop it, you silly boys! (*To* MUFFDIVER.) We were just going out for the day, to the countryside. That's all!

MUFFDIVER: Tsa-Tsa, so why don't we all catch a bit of the seaside then? Get out of the filth.

SYLVIE: But we are the filth, dear. Clint's got a place he fancies.

CLINT: No I haven't.

MUFFDIVER: Yeah? Where is it?

CLINT: I can't go. I gotta buy some shoes today. I start work

46

tomorrow morning.

MUFFDIVER: Right then. We're on. It's a good idea to get out,
with Mr G angry with us and all.

(MUFFDIVER *goes to the door, shouts out.*) Tom-Tom, fancy a
trip?

(SYLVIE *goes to* CLINT *as* MUFFDIVER *organizes the posse.*)

SYLVIE: You look dirty.

CLINT: Thanks.

SYLVIE: I should wash you.

CLINT: You wouldn't.

SYLVIE: I should give you a bath. Come on, Clint.

CLINT: Now?

SYLVIE: Before we go.

INT. BATHROOM. DAY

*The bathroom is a large, dirty room which was once intended to be
luxurious and decadent. A big kidney-shaped bath, with a shelf for
sitting on.*

SYLVIE *has run the water and is testing it with her elbow. She turns
and laughs with* CLINT. *He stands there awkwardly. She grabs his
belt and pulls down his trousers. They struggle. He becomes serious.*

CLINT: What are you doing to me, Sylvie?

Cut to:

INT. BATHROOM. DAY

CLINT *is in the bath washing his hair with shampoo, as she opens a
beer.*

CLINT: Whatever you do, don't look at me.

(*But she looks at him, smiling.*)

Why are you looking like that?

SYLVIE: Don't be afraid of me.

CLINT: (*Holds his arms out*) Look at me.

SYLVIE: You're a beautiful boy.

CLINT: But you wouldn't want to hold my hand, would you?

(*She washes his hair.*)

I'd like to talk to you.

SYLVIE: What would you say, baby?

CLINT: I'd want to know where you've been. I'd love to know
where you come from. Describe your mum and dad.

47

SYLVIE: People who . . . it's incredible . . . the police should stop certain people having children.
CLINT: I hate people who blame their parents for everything.
SYLVIE: So do I.
> (MUFFDIVER *comes into the bathroom and sits down. They look at him nervously but he is abstracted.*)
SYLVIE: (*Embarrassed*) A bath meeting.
Cut to:

INT. BATHROOM. DAY
We see MUFFDIVER *taking his clothes off. The three of them in the bath.* SYLVIE *between* CLINT *and* MUFFDIVER. MUFFDIVER *subdued, dreaming.*
CLINT: (*To* SYLVIE, *of* MUFFDIVER) I like him when he's like this.
SYLVIE: Stoned, or thinking about his money.
> (SYLVIE *and* CLINT *laugh at this.* CLINT *imitates Muffdiver's rage of the previous evening, taking off his voice.*)
CLINT: 'Where's my fucking money, you fucking bastards . . .'
> (*Pause.*) We're the same blood (*To him*) I could touch you, I could. And you could kill me. (*To her*) He could just wipe me out. Maybe he should. I make him feel soft. He hates anyone who does that to him. Even you. I wonder why he wants to be so hard.
> (*She looks at him in surprise.*
> *He quickly gets out of the bath.* SYLVIE *sits there and shivers.*
> CLINT *holds out an old overcoat for her to get into.*)
> Mum, don't get cold.

EXT. OUTSIDE FRONT OF SQUAT. DAY
The posse bundle out of squat, in holiday mood. They've all attempted to dress up for the occasion. They pass DR BUBBA *standing on his balcony, in an elegant white robe, amusedly watching them and casually eating a piece of toast.*
TOM-TOM: (*Mocking*) Om! Om! Om! (*To* BURNS) I've been through all that. Been through it, man!
> (CLINT *is behind them, the last down the stairs, less cheerful than the rest, seeing as* MUFFDIVER's *ruined his day by bringing the whole posse with him.* CLINT *is horrified by* TOM-TOM's *mockery of* DR BUBBA. CLINT *puts his hands together respectfully and bows at* DR BUBBA.)

EXT. RAILWAY STATION. DAY
The posse at Victoria Station running down the platform for a train.
They carry pizzas and beers and TOM-TOM *has a big beat-box with*
him. BURNS *and* CLINT *carry a crate of beer.*
They eventually crash into the compartment of the train, out of breath,
laughing.
The guard blows his whistle. The train starts off from the station.

EXT. COUNTRY STATION. DAY
The posse coming out of a little country station. They are
regarded strangely by passers-by who stop and stare as they stand
blinking in the fresh air. CLINT *spots a bus coming and starts off*
towards it.
MUFFDIVER *put on his dark glasses.*

INT./EXT. BUS. DAY
The posse climb up to the top deck of a country bus, BIKE *having*
difficulty getting his bicycle up the stairs. BURNS *helps him.* SYLVIE
rushes to the front. TOM-TOM *and* CLINT *fight to sit with her,* CLINT
winning, being the more determined.
He turns around to cheer and celebrate but MUFFDIVER *is sitting right*
behind him.
Cut to:

INT. BUS. DAY
The bus speeds through country lanes and suddenly breaks
spectacularly out into open countryside. Cheering.
BURNS: (*Eating*) This is the life.
    (CLINT *shouts at people in the street.*)
CLINT: Get down you leather queens!

EXT. COUNTRYSIDE. DAY
The posse are now standing in open countryside, a little bewildered,
looking lost. They turn to CLINT, *who's the only one with any idea of*
where they are.
Two local kids, a boy and girl of about fifteen or sixteen, stand looking
shyly at them, these London weirdos, in admiration. This is everything
they want to be when they grow up, as cool, bizarre and clearly living
in freedom.
TOM-TOM *waves to them like a rock star greeting his fans.*

49

TOM-TOM: Elmore James. Chuck Berry. The Lightnin' –
   (CLINT *starts off towards the kids.*)
CLINT: Hey, yo, wanna buy something? Need some Ecstasy?
   Acid? Ice?
   (BURNS *grabs him.* BIKE *is laughing.* MUFFDIVER *looks at him
   steadily, neither critically nor with affection but trying to work
   out what's going through his mind. Does* CLINT *really want this
   job? And why has he brought them to this place?*
   BIKE *cycles off down the lane.*
   CLINT *steps over a stile into a field.* TOM-TOM *and* BURNS
   follow him. SYLVIE *takes* MUFFDIVER'S *arm and tries to guide
   him over the stile. He won't go over it.*)
SYLVIE: What's the matter?
MUFFDIVER: My boots. (*And he indicates his superb boots which he
   refuses to get dirty.*)

EXT. COUNTRYSIDE. DAY
*The posse walking through a wood. They're in a cheerful mood – and
drinking. Music from* TOM-TOM's *beat-box.* BURNS *hides behind a
tree and jumps out on* BIKE, *making donkey noises.* MUFFDIVER
*bends over to try and clean his boots, which are already muddy. The
two local kids follow them through the wood, intrigued.*
CLINT: (*To* BIKE) Fancy some country grass?
   (BIKE *takes a spliff.* CLINT *takes one himself.* CLINT *offers one
   to* TOM-TOM. TOM-TOM *waves him away.*)
   This country grass will fly you into the eternal moment.
TOM-TOM: Talk about something else. Foliage. Tree bark. Ten
   years I've been a junkie and I can tell you, druggies are
   boring, small-minded and stupid. The people are enough to
   put you off taking the stuff. Don't you know anything else?
CLINT: I want to, Tom-Tom.
   (MUFFDIVER *takes* SYLVIE's *arm.*)

EXT. POND IN WOOD. DAY
*They walk beside a large pond deep in the woods, watched by the two
local kids from across the other side.* TOM-TOM *wading in the water
by himself, talking to himself.*
TOM-TOM: Otis Redding. (*Pause.*) Marvin Gaye. (*Pause.*)
   Smokey. Smokey Robinson.
   (*Still in dark glasses,* MUFFDIVER *suddenly tries to shove*

BURNS, *who's watching* TOM-TOM, *into the water. He gives him a hard shove but* BURNS *is immovable, as he munches another pizza.*)
BURNS: (*Without turning*) I bet you were a real fucking bully at school.
(TOM-TOM *wades out further.*)
TOM-TOM: Sam Cooke. Bob Marley. Aretha.

EXT. COUNTRYSIDE. DAY
Later. They all walk along a high ridge with a view down to a cottage. In the garden LILY *is hanging out some washing. She has a little boy with her, aged seven or eight.* BURNS *is on the bike,* BIKE *himself beside* BURNS. TOM-TOM *and* MUFFDIVER *together,* MUFFDIVER *nodding as* TOM-TOM *goes on with his list.* SYLVIE *and* CLINT *together, watched by* MUFFDIVER.
CLINT: (*To* SYLVIE) Six months I'd been at the rehab. As a reward, not a punishment, as a reward, they send us on this outward bound shit. We're trudging up a mountain, ten deviants, with four social workers and all.
TOM-TOM: (*Off camera*) J. J. Cale.
CLINT: I've done something wrong and no one's allowed to talk to me. Suddenly I see this carpet of mushrooms, magic mushrooms. They're everywhere, just growing out the earth. I'm behind a tree gobbling them down. Soon the mountain's breathing and the trees are dancing and the sky is swirling with energy and atoms. And I can see the people are sly and cunning and ignorant. I can see that the people who won't let anyone talk to me are in love with power and cruelty. They don't love me. And I know what I want to do. Get back to London and be with the only people for me, having adventures.
TOM-TOM: Phil Spector.
MUFFDIVER: (*Looking at* CLINT) Where's he going . . . with my money?
(*And* CLINT *is running downs the hill towards the cottage, making Red Indian whooping calls.*)
SYLVIE: I think he's spotted a new pair of shoes.

EXT. OUTSIDE COTTAGE. DAY
From LILY's *point of view we see the posse, with* CLINT *running*

down the hill, coming towards her. BIKE *cycles down the hill.* SYLVIE *dances down the hill.*

LILY *is a damaged, nervous woman, smoking constantly, early forties, been through a lot. The cottage has only recently been bought and is in the process of being done up.*

The posse, seen from the house, are a higgedly-piggedly bunch, threatening and risible at the same time.

LILY *examines them closely. She becomes tense and then joyful.*

EXT. FIELD. DAY
LILY *walks and runs towards them.*
LILY: Is it you? Yeah, it would be, it is you!
　　　(*She goes to kiss* CLINT *but* CLINT *holds back, not going to her. We look at* SYLVIE *looking at them, puzzled.*)
CLINT: These are my friends. And this is Sylvie.
LILY: Hallo Muff.
Cut to:

EXT. FRONT OF COTTAGE. DAY
Minutes later, they're all walking towards the cottage, LILY *with her arm around* CLINT.
LILY: (*To* BIKE) We've only had the house a few months.
　　　(*Indicating* CLINT.) I expect he wants to have a look (*Pause.*)
My boy's come back.
　　　(*She turns to look at* MUFFDIVER *who is arguing with* SYLVIE *as they walk.* BURNS *very interested in the house, striding towards it.*)

INT. LILY'S HOUSE/KITCHEN. DAY
LILY *is putting the kettle on. She is with* CLINT. *The others have gone through into the parlour.*
LILY: Don't take this the wrong way – but you haven't come to ask for anything have you?
CLINT: Mum, I've got money.
LILY: Why, what have you and Muff been doing? I can guess.
CLINT: No. Here.
　　　(*He gives her the head he stole from Headley's room.*)
LILY: Thanks. It's dead.
CLINT: It's Japanese. I always bring you something. (*Pause.*) I want a photograph of Dad. Have you still got that one of the three of us?

LILY: I'll have to look for it.
CLINT: Why, haven't you kept much from our old house?
LILY: Some.

INT. PARLOUR. DAY
While LILY *and* CLINT *are in the kitchen, the others have gone through into the parlour,* BIKE *carrying his bicycle of course,* TOM-TOM *soaked,* BURNS *trying to organize them, and* SYLVIE *upset and trying to get heroin out of an irritable* MUFFDIVER. *She pleads with him.*
LILY *and* CLINT *come through with tea.*
LILY: (*To* BIKE.) Wouldn't you like to leave that machine outside?
BURNS: He takes it everywhere with him, love.
LILY: Well, tell him to wipe his tyres.
BURNS: (*To* BIKE.) Wipes your tyres.
        Hallo Muff.
MUFFDIVER: Hallo Lily.
BURNS: There's a cracking fire through there – mind if Tom-Tom gets his clothes off in front of it?
LILY: No, no. My husband'll be back in a minute.
BURNS: How much did you pay for the place, love?
LILY: Dunno.

INT. LILY'S HOUSE. DAY
LILY *is showing them the house. It's been a run down place which she and* STONE *are doing up.* BURNS *touches walls, examines woodwork, electrics, etc.* LILY *perks up at* BURNS'S *interest but keeps looking nervously at* CLINT.
Cut to:

INT. LILY'S HOUSE/VARIOUS ROOMS. DAY
Another room, more finished.
A huge framed poster of Elvis. The only other ornamentation in this room is Elvis paraphernalia – good stuff, well presented, not too tacky.
A photograph of STONE *dressed as Presley which* BIKE *examines and poses as, trying to make* CLINT *laugh – which he doesn't.*
LILY *explaining to* TOM-TOM *what they're doing with the cottage.*
BURNS, CLINT *and* SYLVIE *looking on.*

53

CLINT: Stone'll be back soon. Not my dad – Mum's new
husband. Stoneface.
LILY: Don't you start. He's not new. Eight years we've been
together. (*To* MUFFDIVER.) I wish I'd known you were
coming, Muff.
MUFFDIVER: I wish I'd known, Lily. I thought I was going to the
seaside. Clint, why didn't you say you wanted to see your
mum?
CLINT: Stone – on Saturdays he dresses up as Elvis.
BURNS: I used to do that.
CLINT: Stone hates my guts.
LILY: Have you come home for a slap? Look at the mud on your
feet.
BURNS: When did you get this place?
LILY: We got it a year ago. It was derelict. We've saved it.
BURNS: I bet you're right proud of yourself.
LILY: We've given it all our love and attention.
CLINT: I'm going to have a shower.
BURNS: They haven't got any books.
TOM-TOM: Music says everything I want to know. This place has
music. Listen.
BURNS: I wish I had a house.

INT. KITCHEN. DAY
Later. LILY *goes into the kitchen and finds* SYLVIE *going through the
medicine cupboard, restless and agitated.*
LILY: Headache, love?
(SYLVIE *shakes her head.*)
Need something else?
(LILY *gives her a Valium from her handbag.* LILY *knocks over
an open jar of honey that spreads like an opening flower across the
table.*)
He'll murder me.
SYLVIE: Come on.
(*They clear it up together.*)
SYLVIE: Lily, he's a sweetheart.
LILY: Is he? Yes he is, my little Clint.
SYLVIE: Why –
LILY: His dad was addicted to everything, you name it, and
violent. What he did to me. Someone chopped him up. Good

54

job. What a life – I thought it was over. Then I moved into
John Stone's. You should know, I'll tell you, he loves me.
He has me three times a day. Sometimes more. You can't say
fairer than that. There's no heaven and no God, is there?
SYLVIE: I have to ask. When you went to John Stone's why didn't
you take Clint with you?
LILY: You saying I'd just leave my boy? Stone took him in too.
He was kind to him. And what did Clint do? He puked in
bed. He shouted names at Stone's friends in the Territorial
Army. He injected himself and nearly died. The day came.
Sylvie, I had to choose.
SYLVIE: Between your son and your lover.

EXT. OUTSIDE LILY'S HOUSE. DAY
John STONE, *middle-aged, owns a second-hand shop selling porn,
guns and knives. His dog sits beside him in his car, a pink Cadillac.
He's turned into the yard of his cottage to see* BIKE *doing wheelies.
Further away, sitting on a wall, are the two local kids, watching with
juvenile interest as* BIKE *performs for them.* BIKE *stops when* STONE
turns up.
STONE, *cool, grim, gets out of the car with his dog and walks past*
BIKE *ignoring him.*

INT. KITCHEN. DAY
Through the window LILY *sees* STONE *coming towards the house. She
is nervous.*
LILY: Here he comes now. Please go and calm them all down for
me.
   (SYLVIE *leaves the kitchen.*)
Cut to:

INT. KITCHEN. DAY
John STONE *comes into the kitchen. He steps unwittingly into a pool
of honey which has been overlooked. She looks at him worriedly and
then goes to kiss him.*
STONE: Lily. It's all right.
LILY: Let's have a drink.
   (*She pours two large Scotches.*)

INT. UPSTAIRS CORRIDOR OF COTTAGE. DAY

MUFFDIVER *walks along the top corridor of Stone's house, past a bedroom in which he glimpses* SYLVIE *standing with her back to the door, combing her hair. He goes in and gives her a bag of smack. Another room is the bathroom and* MUFFDIVER *sees his friend* CLINT *leaning against the sink and staring at himself in the mirror. They look at each other in the mirror.*

The last room is Stone's study, a large room. MUFFDIVER *opens the door slowly. The room is full of weapons mounted on the wall: rifles, handguns, antique guns, old swords and daggers.*

The room is also a shrine to Elvis, with Elvis gear everywhere. The room's major item is an Elvis costume, beautifully made, obviously Stone's, mounted on a dummy.

MUFFDIVER *is fascinated by all this stuff and moves further into the room, taking down a dagger and a gun.*

He tries on Stone's Elvis jacket and looks at himself in the full-length mirror, posing with the gun and dagger.

MUFFDIVER: Somebody.

INT. KITCHEN. DAY

STONE *and* LILY *in the kitchen.*

STONE: What's that blackie doing in the yard, love? (*Pause.*) Has your boy come back? For good – or what? What do you want to do with him? Is he the same? Is he?
    (*She gets up. She gestures in distress.*)

INT. STONE'S LIVING ROOM. DAY

STONE *goes into the living room where* TOM-TOM *is fiddling with the piano.* STONE *goes to him.*

STONE: How you keeping?

TOM-TOM: Not well. You?
    (TOM-TOM *plays 'Are You Lonesome Tonight' and* LILY *starts to hum the melody.* STONE *moves snakily, as Presley, impressed by* TOM-TOM's *playing. As* LILY *hums and* TOM-TOM *plays* STONE *does the speaking section of the song, with* BIKE *looking through the window behind him.* BIKE *laughs and urges* TOM-TOM *on. He catches* STONE's *eye.* STONE *gives him a look. Now, as this continues, water starts dripping through the ceiling on to* STONE's *head. He notices. Looks up. And dashes out of the room.*)

56

INT. ROOM IN THE COTTAGE. DAY

STONE *dashes through into another room where* BURNS's *fat carcass is laid out on the sofa, watching TV, a beer and a plate of sandwiches in front of him. As* STONE *dashes through the room to the opposite door,* BURNS *gets up with a sandwich clenched between his teeth, knocking the beer over.*
Cut to:

INT. STAIRCASE/ROOM. DAY

STONE *is going upstairs quickly.*
STONE *is on the top floor of the house. Now he shoves the door of the bedroom and sees* SYLVIE *with her jeans around her knees injecting herself in the crotch.*
In the corridor once more he sees, at the far end, MUFFDIVER *standing guiltily outside the door of* STONE's *study wearing his Elvis jacket.* STONE *jerks his thumbs at him, indicating that he should take it off and get out.* MUFFDIVER *moves.*
Now STONE *bursts into the bathroom and pulls back the shower curtain.* CLINT *is in the shower.*
STONE: Get outta there, boy, the water's coming through.
> (CLINT *jumps out.* STONE *turns off the water, getting wet himself, and several tiles fall off the wall.*)
CLINT: Those tiles must have been stuck up by a moron.
STONE: Jesus. Jesus.
> (STONE *starts throwing the tiles on the floor.* CLINT *is not frightened yet and continues to dry himself, not concealing himself and his eczema-scarred body.* STONE *is shocked rather than hostile.*)
> Someone shove you in an acid bath?
CLINT: I got a job, Stone.
> (STONE *goes slowly towards* CLINT. CLINT *retreats.* STONE *reaches out to touch him.*)
STONE: What kind of strange little boy are you?
CLINT: Don't you touch me.
STONE: Still using shit, Clint? Don't even reply, you're an addict and therefore a complete liar.
> (*Now* SYLVIE *is at the door behind them, not seen by* STONE.)
> Your mother loves you but what you done but break her heart?
CLINT: Have I?
STONE: Apologize to her.

(SYLVIE, *laughing at* STONE, *comes into the room towards him, not in the least scared.*)

SYLVIE: Oh mister. Mister.

(*She goes to* CLINT *and helps him up, holding him.*)

STONE: You're smart, girlie. What you doing with these bad boys? You're above them.

SYLVIE: Me? I'm not above no one.

INT. LIVING ROOM OF COTTAGE. DAY

All the posse present now, in the living room.

LILY *and* BIKE *come into the room carrying tea and biscuits. The atmosphere is no longer relaxed, as it was when they first came into the cottage. They look at each other expectantly, as if to say: 'Should we leave?'*

MUFFDIVER *and* SYLVIE *lie on the sofa together, whispering and playing with each other.*

CLINT *stands there drying his hair after the shower, hurt and disturbed, looking to* MUFFDIVER *for support.* MUFFDIVER *ignores him.*

BURNS *sits forward in an armchair, worried, as always, about all the others.*

TOM-TOM *is at the piano, tinkling a melancholy tune.*

LILY *pours the tea and* BIKE *hands it around to the others.*

LILY: (*To* BIKE) There's a good boy.

(*Now* STONE *comes into the room and stands there, looking at the posse individually, puzzled, as if trying to work out how the posse came to be this way, this loathsome.*

BIKE *hands tea to* BURNS. BURNS *puts his tea down immediately. He's made a decision after seeing* STONE's *face.*)

BURNS: Let's get off then.

STONE: I've said nothing.

BURNS: I can smell . . . (*and he sniffs*) contempt.

STONE: (*Parodying* BURNS's *sniffing*) I'm getting it too. From you. You think everything respectable I've built up with my hands somehow belongs to bums like you. That I don't deserve it. That I've stolen it. I haven't. You people –

BURNS: Here we go.

STONE: You listen for once to someone who isn't stoned, who can speak the English language, fat man. You only desire to be . . . what you are now. This. The lazy dregs of society.

(*Glancing at* MUFFDIVER.) And superior. But none of you
know fuck-all. That boy for instance. (*He indicates* CLINT.) I
know him. Absolutely useless. He knows nothing about
nothing. He can't do fuck-all.
BURNS: (*Shaking his head furiously*) No! There is intelligence –
STONE: You're slaves of sensation, just slaves –
BURNS: Your way of life, that's slavery, habit, repetition –
STONE: Without will or strength or determination. You'll always
take the easy way.
SYLVIE: If only you know, Mr Stone, how hard it is when you're
out of tune with the straight world and what strength and
determination you need when you've got nothing. On the
street . . .
STONE: To tell the truth, girlie, I pity you. I pity people who
don't know the purpose that real work gives you.
BURNS: I can wire a house. I can install a shower.
CLINT: (*To* LILY, *of* STONE) More than he can.
STONE: (*Looking scornfully at* SYLVIE) I saw you upstairs.
Addiction is the most pathetic and wretched thing.
(TOM-TOM *has hung his head during this.* MUFFDIVER *tries to
catch his eye. Tension is rising all round.* MUFFDIVER *shows*
TOM-TOM *the knife.* TOM-TOM *laughs wryly.*)
Because you think you can be happy by sticking a needle in
you. You're yellow cowards, afraid of life.
SYLVIE: (*To* LILY) Lily, when I look at your man, Stone, I think:
that person will never understand anything about other
people's hearts. (*Indicates* CLINT.) Whereas he loves . . .
LILY: (*Shouts*) No, that's a lie. Stone loves! He loves me! (*To*
STONE.) Yes?
STONE: (*To* SYLVIE) If you want to die, go and do it in a corner
and don't commit no crimes on ordinary people.
(STONE *spits on the floor.* MUFFDIVER, *who's been preparing
himself throughout this, hurls himself at* STONE *with his knife.
But* STONE's *a fighter.* MUFFDIVER *and* STONE *struggle,* LILY
screaming, everyone yelling. The knife eventually falls from
MUFFDIVER's *hand.* TOM-TOM *picks it up.*
And BURNS *holds* STONE. SYLVIE *and* CLINT *hold*
MUFFDIVER.
BIKE *turns away.*)
BIKE: (*To* TOM-TOM) I don't think they'll ask us back.

INT. KITCHEN. DAY

BURNS, BIKE, TOM-TOM, SYLVIE *and* MUFFDIVER *going out through the kitchen door.* CLINT, *last, about to follow them, when he spots a pair of shoes parked in the corner of the kitchen, sitting on newspaper, freshly cleaned. He quickly removes his boots and puts on the good shoes, carefully putting the old pair in their place.*

CLINT: The shoe is overdue.

> (*Now he goes through into the hall.*)
>
> Mum.
>
> (*At the top of the stairs he sees the little boy, now in pyjamas and old dressing gown, coming slowly downstairs. At the top of the stairs is* LILY, *preoccupied.*)

LILY: I'm just coming.

EXT. FIELD. AFTERNOON

The posse moves off across the field, SYLVIE *being given a piggy-back by* BURNS.

Now LILY *runs after them, carrying the shoes that* CLINT *left behind. She stops and shouts, running until she catches up with* CLINT.

Seeing this, MUFFDIVER *has the others continue, into the distance.*

LILY: (*Breathless*) Stay, stay. Stone says . . . it's OK.

CLINT: Tomorrow I start work, Mum.

LILY: Whose shoes are those? You left yours. (*She looks down.*)

> Oh no, give them back.
>
> (*He shakes his head.*)
>
> He'll take it out on me. You can't do it! Clint! Thief!
>
> (*She throws the old pair at him.*)

TOM-TOM: Elvis Aaron Presley.

> (*And* STONE *is standing there dressed as Elvis, with a Rottweiler.*)

EXT. COUNTRY STREET. LATE AFTERNOON

An old hippy is coming out of a house with guitar cases, putting them in the back of a big van – watched from across the road by the posse.

MUFFDIVER *looks at* CLINT. CLINT *goes over to the hippy.*

Cut to:

EXT. COUNTRY STREET. LATE AFTERNOON

The van pulls away with them all sitting in the back. We watch this event from the point of view of the two local kids, deeply in awe of the entire event.

Then the van is gone. Music from the beat-box hangs in the air for a while, then silence; desolation. The local kids turn away.

EXT. OUTSIDE THE DINER. NIGHT
Doors of the van burst open. BIKE *cycles out of the van. The others tumble out after him. The hippy's van draws away. The posse on the pavement, dispersing in different directions.*
CLINT *standing outside the diner, watching, ready to wave. He spots* MELANIE. *But at the table she is serving at, he sees Mr G's black* ASSISTANT *and Mr G's two women friends eating and laughing. Now* FAULKNER *crosses the road with one rent boyfriend.*
FAULKNER: So you're back, Marco Polo. Jesus. Phew. You're dead meat, man. All of you.
CLINT: Mr G? He not bothered about us. He amused.
FAULKNER: Not Mr G. Mr Gangster whose place you're squatting. He's heard about it. He's very angry about you sitting on his toilet. He's coming over.
(CLINT *hurries away after the posse.*)

EXT. OUTSIDE THE SHOE SHOP. NIGHT
CLINT *hurries past the shoe shop.* BUSY BEE *in the doorway starts to unpack his paltry belongings and make himself comfortable for the night.*
BUSY BEE: Where's my jumper?

INT. HALLWAY/SUFI CENTRE. NIGHT
CLINT *stands outside the Sufi Centre, watching the chanting and revolving. He catches* DR BUBBA'S *eye and is about to go to him. But* SYLVIE *carrying groceries, is behind him.*
SYLVIE: What a fabulous man, Dr Bubba.
CLINT: But what are they doing, these people? What do they want?
SYLVIE: I talked to one of them. They chant and meditate to get serene. To clear their heads. They want to stop wanting all the time and start really living.
CLINT: Yeah?
(*They remove their shoes and practically dash to join the group. They join the circle and revolve,* CLINT *looking pretty awkward. The others smile and encourage him. He watches* SYLVIE. *After a good whirl, as the circle gets smaller and smaller, they stop, and separate, in a circle.*)

62

DR BUBBA: What do you all feel, if you don't mind? Let us
    compare calmnesses.
    (*There are several replies from the group: 'Yes, calm . . . happy
    . . . OK . . . tired . . . not religious. Not spiritual.'
    Then it's* CLINT's *turn. They look at him.*)
CLINT: Sexy . . . Just . . . sexy.
    (*People freeze, not knowing how to take this. They look at* DR
    BUBBA. DR BUBBA *starts to bend forward and straighten, bend
    and straighten.*)
SYLVIE: (*To someone in group*) He all right?
PERSON IN GROUP: Dr Bubba is doing his laughing meditation.
Cut to:

INT. SUFI CENTRE. NIGHT
SYLVIE *putting on her shoes.* CLINT *looking for his shoes.*
CLINT: Hey, some bloodclaat's swiped my shoes! Hey, yo, Dr
    Bubba, man!
    (*But* DR BUBBA *is talking to someone else.*)
    Where are they! Give them back!
SYLVIE: The shoe has flew!
    (CLINT *starts to smash the place up, throwing things around.*)
CLINT: Where are they! Where are they!
    (DR BUBBA *comes across and removes his own shoes, Indian
    chappals. Very flimsy sandals. He gives them to* CLINT *who is
    very distressed.* CLINT *takes them resentfully.*)

INT. LIVING ROOM OF SQUAT. NIGHT
CLINT *standing in the living room barefoot, waving the sandals
about.* BURNS *playing cards with* BIKE.
CLINT: Look, look! Some religious fucker has stolen my fucking
    shoes!
    (BURNS *replies in German.*)

INT. SQUAT BATHROOM. NIGHT
SYLVIE *is alone in the bathroom. She tries to shut the broken door. She
has cotton wool and a bottle of disinfectant. And a razor blade. She
rolls up her sleeve and slowly, carefully, as if she's done this before –
the dark scars are visible – cuts herself. She cuts herself five times until
the blood comes. She watches herself in the mirror. She bathes each
cut.*

63

INT./ EXT. OUTSIDE BATHROOM DOOR. NIGHT

SYLVIE *comes out of the bathroom.* CLINT *is outside, waiting for her. She is not certain if he's seen her.*

CLINT: Sylvie, what are you doing?

SYLVIE: Don't follow me round.

CLINT: Where are you going now, then?

SYLVIE: Muffdiver's taking me out.

CLINT: Let's go out for a drink first. It's only a few hours before I start work. How about a quick drink?

(*She looks at him and finally relents. He is pleased.*)

INT. HI-TECH BAR. NIGHT

CLINT *and* SYLVIE *go into the hi-tech bar with* BIKE, *minus his bike for a change. The place is pretty full.*

TOM-TOM *is at the bar. A* DWARF *springs around, collecting glasses. As usual, as* CLINT *comes in numerous people talk to him, saying 'Buyin', sellin', got any M-25?' etc.*

CLINT: I'm retired. In a new business. Got a day job.

(CLINT *and* SYLVIE *push through the crowd. Then* CLINT *steps in a puddle of beer, wetting his feet and cursing.*)

DWARF: (*Laughing*) You wanna get some new shoes, innit?
Cut to:

INT. HI-TECH BAR. NIGHT
CLINT *has got them drinks.* SYLVIE *is sitting down, beside*
FAULKNER.
SYLVIE: You love him –
CLINT: I mean it, you an' me, we've got to finish with him. We
    mustn't get dependent.
SYLVIE: But we need him. Look at us, people like us, wasted
    trash –
CLINT: Yes, he'll take us down.
SYLVIE: We can't do nothing for ourselves. He's a sparky little kid
    with a dream.
CLINT: Of money, only. Powerful people, they're the worst, they
    always want to take you over.
FAULKNER: Oh stop it you two.
    (CLINT *stares at her. Kisses her cheek. She sighs. He gets on his
    knees and under the table, between her legs.*)
FAULKNER: Is he?
    (SYLVIE *nods*)
    When he's finished, ask him to do me.
    (*The camera on* SYLVIE'S *face.* FAULKNER *dabs her forehead
    with his handkerchief.*)
Cut to:

INT. HI-TECH BAR. NIGHT
Under the table. We see CLINT *on his knees with his head under*
SYLVIE'S *skirt. As he withdraws for a breather, he notices* FAULKNER'S
excellent shoes which, unlike the rest of him today, are entirely
conventional.
Now SYLVIE *kicks* CLINT *to continue, which he does, while at the same*
time he's clumsily putting one sandalled foot beside FAULKNER'S.
FAULKNER: Lick my toe-caps baby. (*To* SYLVIE.) Clearly no shoe
    is safe in this boy's company.
CLINT: Can I borrow them, Faulkner, just for the day?
FAULKNER: No you can't.
    (*But there's a struggle under the table as* CLINT *frantically tries to*
    wrench FAULKNER'S *shoes off, and* FAULKNER *tries to get rid of*
    him. SYLVIE *laughing.*)

65

Help me, help me!
(*We see* BURNS *and* TOM-TOM *looking at this from across the bar and laughing approvingly.*
BURNS *turns as five or six policemen come into the bar through two entrances.*
As CLINT *comes out from under the table a pint of beer tips off the table and down his back. He gets up quickly, very pissed off, and sees what's happening.*)

CLINT: Oh no, oh Christ, what's happening? They can't arrest me, not now. I'm only a waiter.

SYLVIE: Get rid of your stuff!
(*He stands there petrified, looking around.*)
Clint!
(*Meanwhile everyone in the place reacts fast. They know what to do. We see this in comic detail: people dropping their drugs on the floor; others swallow theirs; a white man, standing beside* TOM-TOM, *drops his stuff into* TOM-TOM's *pocket, even as* TOM-TOM *drops his own stuff on the floor.*
We see feet kicking stuff under tables. One man pops his shit out of the window. Someone else throws a lump of dope in the air and catches it in his mouth.
FAULKNER *punches* CLINT *in the balls.*
SYLVIE *grabs* CLINT *and holds him, going through his pockets, finding his stuff and throwing it on the floor, kicking it under a table into a corner.*)

EXT. OUTSIDE THE HI-TECH BAR IN THE STREET. NIGHT
This isn't a major bust. Two police cars, a couple of arrests. People drifting away.
CLINT *and* SYLVIE *stand to one side, having seen it all before.*
TOM-TOM *is being hauled off by the police.*

CLINT: (*To* TOM-TOM) Sid Vicious.
(CLINT *cracks up laughing.* SYLVIE *nudges him and they see* MUFFDIVER *across the street, dressed up, looking very smart.*)

MUFFDIVER: (*To* SYLVIE) Hi baby. Tsa-Tsa.

SYLVIE: Yeah, look at you, it's nice.
(MUFFDIVER *takes* CLINT *to one side.*)

MUFFDIVER: I'm taking Sylvie out for a bit of grub and then to a little rave. So give me the money you owe me for the hundred and give me the ones you haven't sold.

(CLINT *goes through his pockets.*)
(*Sarcastic.*) Thanks for the day out, man. (*He looks at* CLINT
and is sorry for his sarcasm.) No.
(CLINT *gives him money.*)

CLINT: I had to get rid of the rest of the stuff in there. (*Pause.*) I
won't be working for you no more, Muff, man. I start work
tomorrow.
(MUFFDIVER *looks down at* CLINT's *sandals. Does a double-
take. Looks at him sympathetically.*)

MUFFDIVER: I'll never let something as bad as that happen to you.

CLINT: Have a good evening.
(*He walks away, crying.* MUFFDIVER *yells after him.*)

MUFFDIVER: I won't let them do it to you, I promise, Clint, I won't!

EXT. SQUAT BUILDING. NIGHT

CLINT *walking back to the squat. Outside the house several cars are
parked on the pavement. A* HEAVY *is throwing out the dummies from
Muffdiver's room.*
CLINT *sees the black tramp dressed in rags walking towards him.*
CLINT *runs towards the house.*

INT. HALLWAY/SUFI CENTRE. NIGHT

CLINT *walks upstairs past the door of the Sufi Centre.* DR BUBBA,
who's been waiting to catch him, comes out.

DR BUBBA: Remain down here for some time. Some men are
looking for you boys, courtesy of the previous occupant. They
don't love you.
(*As* CLINT *looks up the stairs, the posse's gear is being thrown out
of the door.* BIKE *suddenly flies down the stairs and is thrown out.
He struggles with the* HEAVY *but is ejected, his bicycle thrown
down after him.
The* HEAVY *turns and glares at* CLINT.)

HEAVY: This squat is closed. You Muffdiver?

CLINT: (*Aggressive*) Why?

HEAVY: Someone's looking for him.

DR BUBBA: (*About* CLINT) This young man is my personal
assistant.
(*The* HEAVY *looks at him and goes. From the top of the stairs we
hear* BURNS *complaining, arguing and fighting with the*
HEAVIES.

67

CLINT *quickly dives back into* DR BUBBA's *place, which is deserted at this time.*

DR BUBBA *watches him walking nervously around the place. He watches him go to the window, open it, and look up at the drainpipe up which he originally entered the house. He starts to climb out of the window.* DR BUBBA *restrains him.*)

Stay here.

CLINT: I had some money for shoes stashed up there. I've gotta get it.

DR BUBBA: They won't let you up, boy. And you must warn your other friends. Don't come back here. Go. Go.

EXT. FRONT OF SQUAT BUILDING. NIGHT

CLINT *is walking quickly away from the squat – backwards. He watches the* HEAVIES *throwing the posse's belongings out into the street.* BURNS *is picking up some of the things and putting them into a supermarket trolley. The* HEAVY *shoves* BURNS *hard and pushes the trolley over.*

CLINT *talks to himself as he turns and runs.*

EXT. DINER. NIGHT

CLINT *walks to the diner and looks in through the window. He sees* MUFFDIVER *and* SYLVIE *sitting at a table eating and talking amicably, drinking wine.*

CLINT *watches them. He can't decide whether to go in or not. He's about to step inside when he sees* HEMINGWAY *putting his coat on and preparing to leave.* MELANIE *is also putting her coat on.*

CLINT *conceals himself as the two of them come out,* MELANIE *putting her arm through* HEMINGWAY's *once they're outside. They go.* CLINT *watches them.*

He turns and BUSY BEE *whose jumper he nicked is standing beside him.*

BUSY BEE: Where's my jumper?

(*Instinctively,* CLINT *turns and runs.*)

INT. HEADLEY'S FLAT. NIGHT

CLINT *is in the hall of Headley's flat, trying to get past her.*

CLINT: Let me in, Headley.

(*He's in a terrible state, exhausted and wretched.*)

HEADLEY: But yesterday you ran out, all independent.

CLINT: Just for a little while.

HEADLEY: To hide from the law. What a gas. Gimme some more of that bush then.

CLINT: I swear I got nothing, Headley.

HEADLEY: What's the point of you then? Got your bloody shoes?
(*She looks at him, in a pitiful state. Then down at his ridiculous sandals and wet feet.*)
What happened to you?

CLINT: It's a long story, Headley.

INT. HEADLEY'S STUDY. NIGHT

HEADLEY *lies face down on her sofa.* CLINT *is brusquely instructed to rub her back.* CLINT *sits over her arse.*

HEADLEY: Ummm . . . yes. There, right, down a bit, harder, move those fingers. Knead my cheeks, darling.

CLINT: I'm not going no further.

HEADLEY: Hey. Don't you need the money?
(*We should play this off* CLINT'*s face; the humiliation, the calculation, the wild thinking and then, with the* MAN'S VOICE, CLINT'*s fear of being beaten up. Suddenly there's an American* MAN'S VOICE *outside and hard knocking on the door.*)

MAN'S VOICE: Headley.

(CLINT *is terrified and looks around for a window to escape through.*)

HEADLEY: How are you, dear? (*To* CLINT.) Don't stop now.

MAN'S VOICE: Am I allowed to come in?

HEADLEY: Goodness, no, I'm not quite ready for you.

MAN'S VOICE: All right if I take a shower then?

(*Pause. The* MAN *goes.* CLINT *gets up.*)

HEADLEY: Stay, stay.

CLINT: I'm not getting into nothing weird. I've been sexually abused before. And I'm starting work tomorrow. I've only got tonight to find a pair of shoes – or get some money to buy some tomorrow morning. Give us some dosh, Headley.

HEADLEY: But you haven't earned it.

CLINT: I beg you, Headley, give us thirty quid, thirty fucking quid, that's all. Give me the money, Headley!

INT. HEADLEY'S FLAT. NIGHT

CLINT *walks quickly through Headley's flat. He sees the man's clothes flung over a chair. But of course he doesn't know they belong to* HEMINGWAY.

Beside the chair is a pair of boots, American boots, tough and colourful and easily distinguishable. The best boots he's seen so far.

CLINT *quickly removes his own Indian chappals and examines these American boots, caressing and sniffing and holding them. He's about to put them on when the door from the shower opens.*

CLINT *scarpers, quickly.*

Cut to:

INT. HEADLEY'S FLAT. NIGHT

HEMINGWAY *comes out of the shower, a towel wrapped around him. He looks down and sees a pair of knackered Indian sandals where his own splendid boots were.*

HEMINGWAY: Headley! Headley! God dammit!

EXT. SHOE SHOP. NIGHT

CLINT *prepares to sleep in the doorway of the shoe shop. A couple of other people are already there, including* BUSY BEE *whose jumper he nicked.*

The others have blankets and rudimentary pillows and stuff, while CLINT *has virtually nothing but an old coat, which he pulls around*

himself, his feet, with the magnificent boots, sticking out. CLINT *spits in his hand and cleans the boots.*
BUSY BEE: Where's my fucking jumper?
CLINT: Tsa-Tsa.

EXT. STREET/NOTTING HILL TUBE. MORNING
The rush hour. Well-dressed, motivated and employed people dash around. CLINT, *eager to join the employed world, moves in and out of the crowd, feeling self-conscious about his wretchedness.*
Across the street BURNS *sees him and calls out.*
BURNS: Clint!
> (*He tries to get through the traffic to* CLINT *but* CLINT *fails to hear him and moves off quickly.*)

EXT. STREET NEAR TUBE AREA. MORNING
CLINT *walking in another part of Notting Hill.* BURNS *has finally caught up with him.*
BURNS: Listen. Christ.
> (BURNS *just grabs him and pulls him off the street.*)
> Come on. This way.
CLINT: Burns, man, I got a job waiting for me. Right now this
> minute.
BURNS: You're with me, little boy, yes you are.
CLINT: No! What are you doing?
> (*But* BURNS *is strong.*)
BURNS: We're going to see the boss, my wee man. And wipe your
> feet too.

EXT/INT. HOTEL. DAY
BURNS *drags* CLINT *through the doors of a seedy hotel in the area.*

INT. HOTEL ROOM. DAY
BURNS *drags* CLINT *into a hotel room, shuts the door and leaves him standing there, a little bewildered.*
MUFFDIVER *and* SYLVIE *are in the room, quite panicky,*
MUFFDIVER *stuffing things into a small bag.* SYLVIE *is getting changed into her Gothess gear.*
The two of them look different, older perhaps, more involved with each other. Still, the atmosphere is tense.
Once more CLINT *feels excluded, but confident about his future.*

71

SYLVIE *and* MUFFDIVER *are warmer towards him than they've ever been, which disconcerts him.*

CLINT: What are you two playing at?

MUFFDIVER: The owner of that squat is looking for us. It's a fact he's very pissed off. So we're going to chill out.

SYLVIE: You should make moves too.

MUFFDIVER: We'll meet somewhere in a few days. We'll rendezvous. In Portsmouth.

CLINT: Portsmouth?

SYLVIE: It's for your sake, baby.

(*Now* MUFFDIVER *puts a long black wig on.* SYLVIE *hands him a black leather studded jacket.*)

MUFFDIVER: I'm disguising myself as Goth in order to leave town without trouble. Sylvie's going as a Gothess.

(*He glances in the mirror at himself. A touch of vanity.* CLINT *can't help laughing at him.*)

CLINT: Yeah, Mr Goth, and I'm starting work in ten minutes time. (*Points.*) Look man, the shoes has come true.

SYLVIE: Sit down. We've got you a birthday present.

(MUFFDIVER *hands him a plastic bag. To his delight* CLINT *pulls out a pair of huge DMs.*)

CLINT: (*To them both*) Thank you. Thanks.

SYLVIE: You're escaping as a skinhead, Clint.

(*She runs her hands through his hair, kisses his cheeks and pulls out a pair of scissors. She starts to cut his hair, cutting out a big lump.*)

CLINT: No! I gotta go. See you!

(*He struggles. She tries to hold him.*)

MUFFDIVER: Be cool, Clint, brother. Put the boots on and get your hair off.

(MUFFDIVER *tries to remove* CLINT'*s boots and replace them with the DMs.*)

CLINT: (*Distressed*) No, you be cool, man. Christ. Sylvie. Christ. Sylvie – I loved you and everything. Both of you. What are you doing? I loved you.

(*And* CLINT *backs away towards the door, trying to stop crying.*)

MUFFDIVER: Clint!

SYLVIE: No! Stay!

(*And* CLINT *dashes out of the door.*)

EXT. STREET. DAY
CLINT *hurries towards the diner, upset, and trying to fix his hair. He stops and tries to look at himself in a mirror on one of the market stalls to see if the missing hank of hair is noticeable. He sees that it is. Walking through the market he steals a cap from a stall he's passing.*
BIKE *stops beside him and shouts at him to stop.*
Then he hurries on, only stopping to check his shoes and adjust the hat. He's ready for HEMINGWAY.

INT. DINER. DAY
The diner is crowded. The two SMART WOMEN *are there, and they recognize Clint. Waiters fly about, including* MELANIE, *who smiles at* CLINT. *Behind the bar the flash barman mixes fantastic cocktails.*
CLINT: (*To* MELANIE) Is Mr Hemingway here?
MELANIE: He expecting you?
CLINT: Oh yeah, Melanie. Tsa-Tsa.
Cut to:

INT. DINER. DAY

CLINT *desperately trying to arrange himself.* HEMINGWAY *emerges.*

CLINT: Here I am, you know, Mr Hemingway, this is me as arranged. The job hasn't gone to another?

> (HEMINGWAY *smiles and shakes his head.*)

HEMINGWAY: Let's have a look at you.

CLINT: (*Turning around*). You know I'm counting on this gig.

> (HEMINGWAY's *eyes start at the top of* CLINT's *body and move slowly downwards. During this process of examination* CLINT *looks out of the window of the diner and sees* MUFFDIVER, *in full heavy Goth gear, standing outside.*)
>
> *With him, also disguised, is* SYLVIE, *with black lipstick, eyeshadow, etc., in long black velvet clothes.*
>
> MUFFDIVER *knocks on the window and indicates for him to come out.*
>
> MELANIE *looks at them and at* CLINT. CLINT *looks away. Then* MUFFDIVER *and* SYLVIE *walk on.*
>
> *Now* HEMINGWAY's *eyes continue. At last he takes in the shoes. And suddenly looks up to* CLINT's *face. He looks down to the boots again, and once more up at* CLINT.
>
> CLINT *smiles broadly, happily, his smile spreading across the screen.*)

CLINT: Whaddya say, Mr Hemingway – the boot is cute, right? The boot is a hoot, yeah?

INT. TRAIN. DAY

MUFFDIVER *is standing in the corridor of a train as it rushes through the English countryside. He is proud, disdainful, and still dressed as a Black Sabbath man.*

SYLVIE *has her head out the window, hair blowing.*

From her point of view we see the countryside rushing away.

EXT. TRAIN IN STATION. DAY

The train has stopped in a station. MUFFDIVER *is now sitting in a seat, looking out of the window. Some of Sylvie's belongings are in the seat next to him. The train starts to move away from the platform. He looks out of the window and sees* SYLVIE *on the platform, walking away from him. She turns and waves. He gets up and gesticulates, but the train is moving away. It is too late. He turns to see her take off her vampire wig and throw it away.*

INT. DINER. DAY
CLINT, *in waiter's gear, subserviently stands by a table, two smart white men in suits are deciding what to eat.* CLINT *has his pad at the ready. As the end titles roll, we see* CLINT *in the restaurant, putting plates down, removing others, running around. Freeze frame on his face.*

Source Music in *London Kills Me*

My job was to find records to be used as source music in the film.

At the first meeting, Hanif gave a general brief: 'I want some records which will give the film an authentic atmosphere; which sound good; and which you like. I don't care where they come from, they could be from Ladbroke Grove, Senegal, Scotland, Louisiana. You tell me.'

When I visit a city for the first time, I love the collage of music that comes at me from all sides, from shop doorways, market stalls, car radios and open windows. I wanted to present a patchwork quilt of London's sounds which an audience would 'believe' without knowing the individual items.

I'm often uncomfortable with scored music; when a composer seeks to enhance the mood of a scene with a deliberate musical gesture, pushing the audience to a particular response, I'm inclined to resent and resist the interference. I prefer the juxtaposition of pictures against a piece of music that already exists, where the changes in the music are done for compositional reasons and there's no self-consciousness in how it connects to the visual action. The skill comes from the editor, adjusting the pictures to the music just enough to make sense of the relationship, but without forcing any unnatural connections.

Over the past twenty years source music has become increasingly prominent in American films. Martin Scorsese made masterly use of records in *Who's That Knocking at my Door* and *Mean Streets*, where pop hits and cult classics from the late fifties and early sixties, alongside older Italian operatic arias, contributed enormously to the films' atmospheres of tension, violence, humour and sadness. Since then, too many films have sacrificed dramatic content to their pop soundtracks, but a special few have made effective use of their records, including *American Graffiti*, *The Last Picture Show*, *The Big Easy*, *Something Wild* and last year's *Goodfellas*, in which Scorsese went back to the era and approach of *Mean Streets*.

In most of those films the records were a nostalgic trigger; they used the music to carry the audience back to the time when they were hits. For *London Kills Me*, I wanted to include records that the audience would not specifically recognize, but would associate with the experience of seeing the film: this is new, now.

I started searching a couple of months before shooting began, while Hanif was auditioning the actors, supervising rehearsals, and attending production meetings. I never know how he found time to listen to the cassettes I bombarded him with, but listen he did, surprising me with his instant grasp of the names, titles and the particular songs he liked.

In the script of *London Kills Me*, there were two obvious contexts for source music: the many scenes in the streets of Notting Hill, and one particular scene at a party, near the beginning of the film. I sorted out a shortlist of about forty current records I felt were roughly right for the film in general, ranging from House through rap and reggae to indie rock, and a few so-called world-music records with what felt like an appropriate mood. Hanif's script included few specific directions for music, but he did have one scene where he hoped for what he called 'much third worldism'; in the end, that particular scene was cut out of the film; bye bye Youssou, so long Mari Boine.

As I skirted around records which featured the most blatant dance hit formulas of the time – James Brown vocal samples, wailing female vocals, percussive piano chords – a common thread began to emerge among the surviving contenders, with influences of jazz and/or reggae giving a warmer, more musical touch to even the toughest dance tracks.

For the party I was determined to avoid a problem that afflicts many films, where a scene is shot of people dancing to a convenient hit, which is later substituted by something different on the film soundtrack: it's impossible for the editor to synchronize the dancers' movements to the music. I wanted live DJ's at the party to play an agreed repertoire of contractually available records, so we could use the same music on the soundtrack. Ben Peel and Marc Pettifore run warehouse raves in south London which cover the gamut of modern dance music. We sifted through our combined collections, homing in on records which met all the criteria, by artists including Bass-O-Matic, Daddy Freddy, Definition of Sound, Djum Djum, Flourgon and Ninjanan, Izit, JCOOl and D*Zire, LeftField, Man Machine, Massive Attack, Michael Prophet and Ricky Tuffy, the Raga Twins, Renegade Soundwave,

St Etienne with Q-T. As it turned out, for continuity reasons only four records were played throughout the day at the party, but the selection process was invaluable in confirming the range and mood of music that suited the film.

I wanted to include some kind of 'rock' following the trail left by Big Audio Dynamite, the Notting Hill-based group formed by Mick Jones of the Clash with ex-film-maker Don Letts, who brought a reggae touch to the group's powerful rock approach. Hanif felt their music would unbalance the film with too many specific associations, and we found our answer in the album *In Dub* by Renegade Soundwave, a trio based in Notting Hill who fuse rock guitar and reggae bass over slow but consistent dance grooves. The film opens to the dramatic sound of Renegade Soundwave's instrumental mix of 'Biting My Nails', whose episodic structure seems tailor-made for a film score.

At the end of each day's shoot, the film would be rushed to the labs for developing, and the next day editor Jon Gregory assembled the material into its scripted sequence, so that within a day of the end of shooting, he had the whole film loosely edited together. A video copy was made, and Hanif and I began to assign various records to particular spots where they seemed to fit. The decisions were mostly quite easy: some scenes were immediately enhanced, other felt uncomfortable. When in doubt we left it out, deciding that either the scene didn't need music at all, or that sparse scored music might suit it better.

We transferred the likely contenders to magnetic tape, and Jon Gregory began to edit the film to the particular items we'd chosen. The process of elimination then took several months, as each piece we included affected the scenes around it. Sometimes Jon found a better context for a piece of music than the place Hanif and I had chosen, notably 'Mustt Mustt' by Nusrat Fateh Ali Khan. Changes were being made right up to the finish, and five pieces which had been apparent certainties for several weeks were dropped on the last possible day. Hanif, Jon and I had remarkably few disagreements about what worked or didn't work. We all had regrets about songs we hoped to include but couldn't find an appropriate place for; but the film had to win, over our individual emotional preferences.

Charlie Gillett
London, 1991

79

Music End Credits

1. *Biting My Nails* by Renegade Soundwave (Mute Records)
2. *Zig It Up* by Ninjaman and Flourgon (Jet Star Records)
3. *Soul Surrender* by Bass-O-Matic (Virgin Records)
4. *More Than I Know* by LeftField (Outer Rhythm Records)
5. *Guayacil City* by Mano Negra (Virgin Records)
6. *Pocket Porn Dub* by Renegade Soundwave (Mute Records)
7. *Baina Nakhill* by Hassan Erraji (Riverboat Records)
8. *Your Love* by Michael Prophet and Ricky Tuffy (Passion Records)
9. *Mustt Mustt* by Nusrat Fateh Ali Khan (Real World Records)
10. *Beautiful People* by Stress (Eternal Records)
11. *Step Into Time* by Man Machine (Outer Rhythm Records)
12. *Are You Lonesome Tonight?* © Redwood Music and Bourne Music
13. *Make Way for the Originals* by Izit (Pig and Trumpet Records)
14. *Fast Fish and Loose Fish* (The Bone Mix) by QRZ (10 records)
15. *Rising Above Bedlam* by Jah Wobble's Invaders of the Heart (Oval Records)
16. *The Pleasure and the Pain* by Debby Browne (Oval Records)

Eight Arms to Hold You

One day at school – an all-boys comprehensive on the border between London and Kent – our music teacher told us that John Lennon and Paul McCartney didn't actually write those famous Beatles songs we loved so much.

It was 1968 and I was thirteen. For the first time in music appreciation class we were to listen to the Beatles – 'She's Leaving Home', with the bass turned off. The previous week, after some Brahms, we'd been allowed to hear a Frank Zappa record, again bassless. For Mr Hogg, our music and religious instruction teacher, the bass guitar 'obscured' the music. But hearing anything by the Beatles at school was uplifting, an act so unusually liberal it was confusing.

Mr Hogg prised open the lid of the school 'stereophonic equipment', which was kept in a big, dark wooden box and wheeled around the premises by the much-abused war-wounded caretaker. Hogg put on 'She's Leaving Home' without introduction, but as soon as it began he started his Beatles analysis.

What he said was devastating, though it was put simply, as if he were stating the obvious. These were the facts: Lennon and McCartney could not possibly have written the songs ascribed to them; it was a con – we should not be taken in by the 'Beatles', they were only front-men.

Those of us who weren't irritated by his prattling through the tune were giggling. Certainly, for a change, most of us were listening to teacher. I was perplexed. Why would anyone want to think anything so ludicrous? What was really behind this idea?

'Who did write the Beatles' songs, then, sir?' someone asked bravely. And Paul McCartney sang:

> We struggled hard all our lives to get by,
> She's leaving home after living alone,
> For so many years.

Mr Hogg told us that Brian Epstein and George Martin wrote the Lennon/McCartney songs. The Fabs only played on the records – if they did anything at all. (Hogg doubted whether their hands had actually touched the instruments.) 'Real musicians were playing on those records,' he said. Then he put the record back in its famous sleeve and changed the subject.

But I worried about Hogg's theory for days; on several occasions I was tempted to buttonhole him in the corridor and discuss it further. The more I dwelt on it alone, the more it revealed. The Mopheads couldn't even read music – how could they be geniuses?

It was unbearable to Mr Hogg that four young men without significant education could be the bearers of such talent and critical acclaim. But then Hogg had a somewhat holy attitude to culture. 'He's cultured,' he'd say of someone, the antonym of 'He's common.' Culture, even popular culture – folk-singing, for instance – was something you put on a special face for, after years of wearisome study. Culture involved a particular twitching of the nose, a faraway look (into the sublime), and a fruity pursing of the lips. Hogg knew. There was, too, a sartorial vocabulary of knowingness, with leather patches sewn on to the elbows of shiny, rancid jackets.

Obviously this was not something the Beatles had been born into. Nor had they acquired it in any recognized academy or university. No, in their early twenties, the Fabs made culture again and again, seemingly without effort, even as they mugged and winked at the cameras like schoolboys.

Sitting in my bedroom listening to the Beatles on a Grundig reel-to-reel tape-recorder, I began to see that to admit to the Beatles' genius would devastate Hogg. It would take too much else away with it. The songs that were so perfect and about recognizable common feelings – 'She Loves You', 'Please, Please Me', 'I Wanna Hold Your Hand' – were all written by Brian Epstein and George Martin because the Beatles were only boys like us: ignorant, bad-mannered and rude; boys who'd never, in a just world, do anything interesting with their lives. This implicit belief, or form of contempt, was not abstract. We felt and sometimes recognised – and Hogg's attitude towards the Beatles exemplified this – that our teachers had no respect for us as people capable of learning, of finding the world compelling and wanting to know it.

The Beatles would also be difficult for Hogg to swallow because for him there was a hierarchy among the arts. At the top were stationed classical music and poetry, beside the literary novel and great painting. In the middle would be not-so-good examples, of these forms. At the bottom of the list, and scarcely considered art forms at all, were films ('the pictures'), television and, finally, the most derided – pop music.

But in that post-modern dawn – the late 1960s – I like to think that Hogg was starting to experience cultural vertigo – which was why he worried about the Beatles in the first place. He thought he knew what culture was, what counted in history, what had weight, and what you needed to know to be educated. These things were not relative, not a question of taste or decision. Notions of objectivity did exist; there were criteria and Hogg knew what the criteria were. Or at least he thought he did. But that particular form of certainty, of intellectual authority, along with many other forms of authority, was shifting. People didn't know where they were any more.

Not that you could ignore the Beatles even if you wanted to. Those rockers in suits were unique in English popular music, bigger than anyone had been before. What a pleasure it was to swing past Buckingham Palace in the bus knowing the Queen was indoors, in her slippers, watching her favourite film, *Yellow Submarine*, and humming along to 'Eleanor Rigby'. ('All the lonely people . . .')

The Beatles couldn't be as easily dismissed as the Rolling Stones, who often seemed like an ersatz American group, especially when Mick Jagger started to sing with an American accent. But the Beatles' music was supernaturally beautiful and it was English music. In it you could hear cheeky music-hall songs and send-ups, pub ballads and, more importantly, hymns. The Fabs had the voices and looks of choirboys, and their talent was so broad they could do anything – love songs, comic songs, kids' songs and sing-alongs for football crowds (at White Hart Lane, Tottenham Hotspurs' ground, we sang: 'Here, there and every-fucking-where, Jimmy Greaves, Jimmy Greaves'). They could do rock 'n' roll too, though they tended to parody it, having mastered it early on.

One lunch-time in the school library, not long after the incident with Hogg, I came across a copy of *Life* magazine which included hefty extracts from Hunter Davies's biography of the Beatles, the first major book about them and their childhood. It was soon stolen from the library and passed around the school, a contemporary 'Lives of the Saints'. (On the curriculum we were required to read Gerald Durrell and C. S. Forester, but we had our own books, which we discussed, just as we exchanged and discussed records. We liked *Candy*, *Lord of the Flies*, James Bond, Mervyn Peake, and *Sex Manners for Men*, among other things.)

Finally my parents bought the biography for my birthday. It was the first hardback I possessed and, pretending to be sick, I took the day off school to read it, with long breaks between chapters to prolong the pleasure. But *The Beatles* didn't satisfy me as I'd imagined it would. It wasn't like listening to *Revolver*, for instance, after which you felt satisfied and uplifted. The book disturbed and intoxicated me; it made me feel restless and dissatisfied with my life. After reading about the Beatles' achievements I began to think I didn't expect enough of myself, that none of us at school did really. In two years we'd start work; soon after that we'd get married and buy a small house nearby. The form of life was decided before it was properly begun.

To my surprise it turned out that the Fabs were lower-middle-class provincial boys; neither rich nor poor, their music didn't come out of hardship and nor were they culturally privileged. Lennon was rough, but it wasn't poverty that made him hard-edged. The Liverpool Institute, attended by Paul and George, was a good grammar school. McCartney's father had been well enough off for Paul and his brother Michael to have piano lessons. Later, his father bought him a guitar.

We had no life guides or role models among politicians, military types or religious figures, or even film stars for that matter, as our parents did. Footballers and pop stars were the revered figures of my generation and the Beatles, more than anyone, were exemplary for countless young people. If coming from the wrong class restricts your sense of what you can be, then none of us thought we'd become doctors, lawyers, scientists, politicians. We were scheduled to be clerks, civil servants, insurance managers and travel agents.

Not that leading some kind of creative life was entirely impossible. In the mid-1960s the media was starting to grow.

There was a demand for designers, graphic artists and the like. In our art lessons we designed toothpaste boxes and record sleeves to prepare for the possibility of going to art school. Now, these were very highly regarded among the kids; they were known to be anarchic places, the sources of British pop art, numerous pop groups and the generators of such luminaries as Pete Townshend, Keith Richards, Ray Davies and John Lennon. Along with the Royal Court and the drama corridor of the BBC, the art schools were the most important post-war British cultural institution, and some lucky kids escaped into them. Once, I ran away from school to spend the day at the local art college. In the corridors where they sat cross-legged on the floor, the kids had dishevelled hair and paint-splattered clothes. A band was rehearsing in the dining hall. They liked being there so much they stayed till midnight. Round the back entrance there were condoms in the grass.

But these kids were destined to be commercial artists, which was, at least, 'proper work'. Commercial art was OK but anything that veered too closely towards pure art caused embarrassment; it was pretentious. Even education fell into this trap. When, later, I went to college, our neighbours would turn in their furry slippers and housecoats to stare and tut-tut to each other as I walked down the street in my Army-surplus greatcoat, carrying a pile of library books. I like to think it was the books rather than the coat they were objecting to – the idea that they were financing my uselessness through their taxes. Surely nurturing my brain could be of no possible benefit to the world; it would only render me more argumentative – create an intelligentsia and you're only producing criticism for the future.

(For some reason I've been long under the impression that this hatred for education is a specifically English tendency. I've never imagined the Scots, Irish or Welsh, and certainly no immigrant group, hating the idea of elevation through the mind in quite the same way. Anyhow, it would be a couple of decades before the combined neighbours of south-east England could take their revenge on education via their collective embodiment – Thatcher.)

I could, then, at least have been training to be an apprentice. But, unfortunately for the neighbours, we had seen *A Hard Day's Night* at Bromley Odeon. Along with our mothers, we screamed all through it, fingers stuck in our ears. And afterwards we didn't know what to do with ourselves, where to go, how to exorcize this passion the Beatles had stoked up. The ordinary wasn't enough; we couldn't accept only the everyday now! We desired ecstasy, the extraordinary, magnificence – today!

For most, this pleasure lasted only a few hours and then faded. But for others it opened a door to the sort of life that might, one day, be lived. And so the Beatles came to represent opportunity and possibility. They were careers officers, a myth for us to live by, a light for us to follow.

How could this be? How was it that of all the groups to emerge from that great pop period the Beatles were the most dangerous, the most threatening, the most subversive? Until they met Dylan and, later, dropped acid, the Beatles wore matching suits and wrote harmless love songs offering little ambiguity and no call to rebellion. They lacked Elvis's sexuality, Dylan's introspection and Jagger's surly danger. And yet . . . and yet – this is the thing – everything about the Beatles represented pleasure, and for the provincial and suburban young pleasure was only the outcome and justification of work. Pleasure was work's reward and it occurred only at weekends and after work.

But when you looked at *A Hard Day's Night* or *Help!*, it was clear that those four boys were having the time of their life: the films radiated freedom and good times. In them there was no sign of the long, slow accumulation of security and status, the year-after-year movement towards satisfaction, that we were expected to ask of life. Without conscience, duty or concern for the future, everything about the Beatles spoke of enjoyment, abandon and attention to the needs of the self. The Beatles became heroes to the young because they were not deferential: no authority had broken their spirit; they were confident and funny; they answered back; no one put them down. It was this independence, creativity and earning-power that worried Hogg about the Beatles. Their naïve hedonism and dazzling accomplishments were too paradoxical. For Hogg to wholeheartedly approve of them was like saying crime paid. But to dismiss the new world of the 1960s was to admit to being old and out of touch.

There was one final strategy that the defenders of the straight world developed at this time. It was a common stand-by of the neighbours. They argued that the talent of such groups was shallow. The easy money would soon be spent, squandered on objects the groups would be too jejune to appreciate. These musicians couldn't think about the future. What fools they were to forfeit the possibility of a secure job for the pleasure of having teenagers worship them for six months.

This sneering 'anyone-can-do-it' attitude to the Beatles wasn't necessarily a bad thing. Anyone could have a group – and they did. But it was obvious from early on that the Beatles were not a two-hit group like the Merseybeats or Freddie and the Dreamers. And around the time that Hogg was worrying about the authorship of 'I Saw Her Standing There' and turning down the bass on 'She's Leaving Home', just as he was getting himself used to them, the Beatles were doing something that had never been done before. They were writing songs about drugs, songs that could be fully comprehended only by people who took drugs, songs designed to be enjoyed all the more if you were stoned when you listened to them.

And Paul McCartney had admitted to using drugs, specifically LSD. This news was very shocking then. For me, the only association that drugs conjured up was of skinny Chinese junkies in squalid opium dens and morphine addicts in B movies; there had also been the wife in *Long Day's Journey into Night*. What were the Mopheads doing to themselves? Where were they taking us?

On Peter Blake's cover for *Sgt Pepper*, between Sir Robert Peel and Terry Southern, is an ex-Etonian novelist mentioned in *Remembrance of Things Past* and considered by Proust to be a genius – Aldous Huxley. Huxley first took mescalin in 1953, twelve years before the Beatles used LSD. He took psychedelic drugs eleven times, including on his death bed, when his wife injected him with LSD. During his first trip Huxley felt himself turning into four bamboo chair legs. As the folds of his grey flannel trousers became 'charged with is-ness' the world became a compelling, unpredictable, living and breathing organism. In this transfigured universe Huxley realized both his fear of and need for the 'marvellous'; one of the soul's principal appetites was for 'transcendence'. In an alienated, routine world ruled by habit, the urge for escape, for euphoria, for heightened sensation, could not be denied.

Despite his enthusiasm for LSD, when Huxley took psilocybin

with Timothy Leary at Harvard he was alarmed by Leary's ideas about the wider use of psychedelic drugs. He thought Leary was an 'ass' and felt that LSD, if it were to be widely tried at all, should be given to the cultural élite – to artists, psychologists, philosophers and writers. It was important that psychedelic drugs be used seriously, primarily as aids to contemplation. Certainly they changed nothing in the world, being 'incompatible with action and even with the will to action'. Huxley was especially nervous about the aphrodisiac qualities of LSD and wrote to Leary: 'I strongly urge you not to let the sexual cat out of the bag. We've stirred up enough trouble suggesting that drugs can stimulate aesthetic and religious experience.'

But there was nothing Huxley could do to keep the 'cat' in the bag. In 1961 Leary gave LSD to Allen Ginsberg, who became convinced the drug contained the possibilities for political change. Four years later the Beatles met Ginsberg through Bob Dylan. At his own birthday party Ginsberg was naked apart from a pair of underpants on his head and a 'do not disturb' sign tied to his penis. Later, Lennon was to learn a lot from Ginsberg's style of self-exhibition as protest, but on this occasion he shrank from Ginsberg, saying: 'You don't do that in front of the birds!'

Throughout the second half of the 1960s the Beatles functioned as that rare but necessary and important channel, popularizers of esoteric ideas – about mysticism, about different forms of political involvement and about drugs. Many of these ideas originated with Huxley. The Beatles could seduce the world partly because of their innocence. They were, basically, good boys who became bad boys. And when they became bad boys, they took a lot of people with them.

Lennon claimed to have 'tripped' hundreds of times, and he was just the sort to become interested in unusual states of mind. LSD creates euphoria and suspends inhibition; it may make us aware of life's intense flavour. In the tripper's escalation of awareness, the memory is stimulated too. Lennon knew the source of his art was the past, and his acid songs were full of melancholy, self-examination and regret. It's no surprise that *Sgt Pepper*, which at one time was to include 'Strawberry Fields' and 'Penny Lane', was originally intended to be an album of songs about Lennon and McCartney's Liverpool childhood.

Soon the Beatles started to wear clothes designed to be read by people who were stoned. God knows how much 'is-ness' Huxley would have felt had he seen John Lennon in 1967, when he was reportedly wearing a green flower-patterned shirt, red cord trousers, yellow socks and a sporran in which he carried his loose change and keys. These weren't the cheap but hip adaptations of work clothes that young males had worn since the late 1940s – Levi jackets and jeans, sneakers, work boots or DMs, baseball caps, leather jackets – democratic styles practical for work. The Beatles had rejected this conception of work. Like Baudelairean dandies they could afford to dress ironically and effeminately, for each other, for fun, beyond the constraints of the ordinary. Stepping out into that struggling post-war world steeped in memories of recent devastation and fear – the war was closer to them than *Sgt Pepper* is to me today – wearing shimmering bandsman's outfits, crushed velvet, peach-coloured silk and long hair, their clothes were gloriously non-functional, identifying their creativity and the pleasures of drug-taking.

By 1966 the Beatles behaved as if they spoke directly to the whole world. This was not a mistake: they were at the centre of life for millions of young people in the West. And certainly they're the only mere pop group you could remove from history and suggest that culturally, without them, things would have been significantly different. All this meant that what they did was influential and important. At this time, before people were aware of the power of the media, the social changes the Beatles sanctioned had happened practically before anyone noticed. Musicians have always been involved with drugs, but the Beatles were the first to parade their particular drug-use – marijuana and LSD – publicly and without shame. They never claimed, as musicians do now – when found out – that drugs were a 'problem' for them. And unlike the Rolling Stones, they were never humiliated for drug-taking or turned into outlaws. There's a story that at a bust at Keith Richard's house in 1967, before the police went in they waited for George Harrison to leave. The Beatles made taking drugs seem an enjoyable, fashionable and liberating experience: like them, you would see and feel in ways you hadn't imagined possible. Their endorsement, far more than that of any other group or individual, removed drugs from their sub-cultural, avant-garde and generally squalid associations, making them part of mainstream youth activity. Since then, illegal drugs have accompanied music, fashion and dance as part of what it is to be young in the West.

Allen Ginsberg called the Beatles 'the paradigm of the age', and they were indeed condemned to live out their period in all its foolishness, extremity and commendable idealism. Countless preoccupations of the time were expressed through the Fabs. Even Apple Corps was a characteristic 1960s notion: an attempt to run a business venture in an informal, creative and non-materialistic way.

Whatever they did and however it went wrong, the Beatles were always on top of things musically, and perhaps it is this, paradoxically, that made their end inevitable. The loss of control that psychedelic drugs can involve, the political anger of the 1960s and its anti-authoritarian violence, the foolishness and inauthenticity of being pop stars at all, rarely violates the highly finished surface of their music. Songs like 'Revolution' and 'Helter Skelter' attempt to express unstructured or deeply felt passions, but the Beatles are too controlled to let their music fray. It never felt as though the band was going to disintegrate through sheer force of feeling, as with Hendrix, the Who or the Velvet Underground. Their ability was so extensive that all madness could be contained within a song. Even 'Strawberry Fields' and 'I Am the Walrus' are finally engineered and controlled. The exception is 'Revolution No.9', which Lennon had to fight to keep on the *White Album*; he wanted to smash through the organization and accomplished form of his pop music. But Lennon had to leave the Beatles to continue in that direction and it wasn't until his first solo album that he was able to strip away the Beatle frippery for the raw feeling he was after.

At least, Lennon wanted to do this. In the 1970s, the liberation tendencies of the 1960s bifurcated into two streams – hedonism, self-aggrandisement and decay, represented by the Stones; and serious politics and self-exploration, represented by Lennon. He continued to be actively involved in the obsessions of the time, both as initiate and leader, which is what makes him the central cultural figure of the age, as Brecht was, for instance, in the 1930s and 1940s.

But to continue to develop Lennon had to leave the containment of the Beatles and move to America. He had to break up the Beatles to lead an interesting life.

I heard a tape the other day of a John Lennon interview. What struck me, what took me back irresistibly, was realizing how much I loved his voice and how inextricably bound up it was with my own growing up. It was a voice I must have heard almost everyday for years, on television, radio or record. It was more exceptional then than it is now, not being the voice of the BBC or of southern England, or of a politician; it was neither emollient nor instructing, it was direct and very hip. It pleased without trying to. Lennon's voice continues to intrigue me, and not just for nostalgic reasons, perhaps because of the range of what it says. It's a strong but cruel and harsh voice; not one you'd want to hear putting you down. It's naughty, vastly melancholic and knowing too, full of self-doubt, self-confidence and humour. It's expressive, charming and sensual; there's little concealment in it, as there is in George Harrison's voice, for example. It is aggressive and combative but the violence in it is attractive since it seems to emerge out of a passionate involvement with the world. It's the voice of someone who is alive in both feeling and mind; it comes from someone who has understood their own experience and knows their value.

The only other public voice I know that represents so much, that seems to have spoken relentlessly to me for years, bringing with it a whole view of life – though from the dark side – is that of Margaret Thatcher. When she made her 'St Francis of Assisi' speech outside 10 Downing Street after winning the 1979 General Election, I laughed aloud at the voice alone. It was impenetrable to me that anyone could have voted for a sound that was so cold, so pompous, so clearly insincere, ridiculous and generally absurd.

In this same voice, and speaking of her childhood, Thatcher once said that she felt that 'To pursue pleasure for its own sake was wrong'.

In retrospect it isn't surprising that the 1980s *mélange* of liberal economics and Thatcher's pre-war Methodist priggishness would embody a reaction to the pleasure-seeking of the 1960s and 1970s, as if people felt ashamed, guilty and angry about having gone too far, as if they'd enjoyed themselves too much. The greatest surprise was had by the Left – the ideological left rather than the pragmatic Labour Party – which believed it had, during the 1970s, made immeasurable progress since *Sgt Pepper*, penetrating the media and the Labour Party, the universities and the law, fanning out and reinforcing itself in various organizations like the gay, black and women's movements. The 1960s was a romantic period and Lennon a great romantic hero, both as poet and political icon. Few thought that what he represented would all end so quickly and easily, that the Left would simply hand over the moral advantage and their established positions in the country as if they hadn't fought for them initially.

Thatcher's trope against feeling was a resurrection of control, a repudiation of the sensual, of self-indulgence in any form, self-exploration and the messiness of non-productive creativity, often specifically targeted against the 'permissive' 1960s. Thatcher's colleague Norman Tebbit characterized this suburban view of the Beatle period with excellent vehemence, calling it: 'The insufferable, smug, sanctimonious, naïve, guilt-ridden, wet, pink orthodoxy of that sunset home of that third-rate decade, the 60s.'

The amusing thing is that Thatcher's attempt to convert Britain to an American-style business-based society has failed. It is not something that could possibly have taken in such a complacent and divided land, especially one lacking a self-help culture. Only the immigrants in Britain have it: they have much to fight for and much to gain through being entrepreneurial. But it's as if no one else can be bothered – they're too mature to fall for such ideas.

Ironically, the glory, or, let us say, the substantial achievements of Britain in its ungracious decline, has been its art. There is here a tradition of culture dissent (or argument or cussedness) caused by the disaffections and resentments endemic in a class-bound society, which fed the best fiction of the 1960s, the theatre of the 1960s and 1970s, and the cinema of the early 1980s. But principally and more prolifically, reaching a world-wide audience and being innovative and challenging, there is the production of pop music – the richest cultural form of post-war Britain. Ryszard Kapuscinski in 'Shah of Shahs' quotes a Tehran carpet salesman: 'What have we given the world? We have given poetry, the miniature, and carpets. As you can see, these are all useless things from the productive viewpoint. But it is through such things that we have expressed our true selves.'

The Beatles are the godhead of British pop, the hallmark of excellence in song-writing and, as importantly, in the interweaving of music and life. They set the agenda for what was possible in pop music after them. And Lennon, especially, in refusing to be a career pop star and dissociating himself from the politics of his time, saw, in the 1970s, pop becoming explicitly involved in social issues. In 1976 Eric Clapton interrupted a concert he was giving in Birmingham to make a speech in support of Enoch Powell. The incident led to the setting up of Rock Against Racism. Using pop music as an instrument of solidarity, as resistance and propaganda, it was an effective movement against the National Front at a time when official politics – the Labour Party – were incapable of taking direct action around immediate street issues. And punk too, of course, emerged partly out of the unemployment, enervation and directionlessness of the mid-1970s.

During the 1980s, Thatcherism discredited such disinterested and unprofitable professions as teaching, and yet failed, as I've said, to implant a forging culture of self-help. Today, as then, few British people believe that nothing will be denied them if only they work hard enough, as many Americans, for instance, appear to believe. Most British know for a fact that, whatever they do, they can't crash through the constraints of the class system and all the prejudices and instincts for exclusion that it contains. But pop music is the one area in which this belief in mobility, reward and opportunity does exist.

Fortunately the British school system can be incompetent, liberal and so lacking in self-belief that it lacks the conviction to crush the creativity of young people, which does, therefore, continue, to flourish in the interstices of authority, in the school corridor and after four o'clock, as it were. The crucial thing is to have education that doesn't stamp out the desire to learn, that attempts to educate while the instincts of young people – which desire to be stimulated but in very particular things, like sport, pop music and television – flower in spite of the teacher's requirement to educate. The sort of education that Thatcherism needed as a base – hard-line, conformist, medicinal, providing soldiers for the trenches of business wars and not education for its own sake – is actually against the tone or feeling of an England that is not naturally competitive, not being desperate enough, though desperate conditions were beginning to be created.

Since Hogg first played 'She's Leaving Home', the media has

expanded unimaginably, but pop music remains one area accessible to all, both for spectators and, especially, for participants. The cinema is too expensive, the novel too refined and exclusive, the theatre too poor and middle-class, and television too complicated and rigid. Music is simpler to get into. And pop musicians never have to ask themselves – in the way that writers, for instance, constantly have to – who is my audience, who am I writing for and what am I trying to say? It is art for their own sakes, and art which connects with a substantial audience hungry for a new product, an audience which is, by now, soaked in the history of pop music and is sophisticated, responsive and knowledgeable.

And so there has been in Britain since the mid-1960s a stream of fantastically accomplished music, encompassing punk and New Wave, northern soul, reggae, hip-hop, rap, acid jazz and house. The Left, in its puritanical way, has frequently dismissed pop as capitalist pap, preferring folk and other 'traditional' music. But it is pop that has spoken of ordinary experience with far more precision, real knowledge and wit than, say, British fiction of the equivalent period. And you can't dance to fiction.

In the 1980s, during Thatcher's 'permanent revolution', there was much talk of identity, race, nationality, history and, naturally, culture. But pop music, which has bound young people together more than anything else, was usually left out. But this tradition of joyous and lively music created by young people from state schools, kids from whom little was expected, has made a form of self-awareness, entertainment and effective criticism that deserves to be acknowledged and applauded but never institutionalized. But then that is up to the bands and doesn't look like happening, pop music being a rebellious form in itself if it is to be any good. And the Beatles, the most likely candidates ever for institutionalization, finally repudiated that particular death through the good sense of John Lennon, who gave back his MBE, climbed inside a white bag and wrote 'Cold Turkey'.

Hanif Kureishi
1991

94

Faber Screenplays

If you have enjoyed this book, then take a look at the following:

MY BEAUTIFUL LAUNDRETTE with THE RAINBOW SIGN

The most popular British film of the eighties, together with Kureishi's extended autobiographical essay about growing up in a racist society.

SAMMY AND ROSIE GET LAID

Kureishi's second film takes a look at the disintegration of the old morality during the Thatcher years. With an exclusive diary about the making of the film.

SEX, LIES AND VIDEOTAPE

How did a first time director get to win the most coveted prize in the film industry, the Palme d'Or at Cannes? Steven Soderbergh explains how, together with the screenplay that launched his career.

AU REVOIR LES ENFANTS and LACOMBE, LUCIEN

Louis Malle's two films set during the war and French occupation, the first about a collaborator, the second a passionate recreation of a boyhood friendship. With an Introduction by Philip French.

DECALOGUE (including A SHORT FILM ABOUT KILLING and A SHORT FILM ABOUT LOVE)

Krzysztof Kieślowski's remarkable sequence of films based on the Ten Commandments also includes an Introduction by Kieślowski about his career and a Foreword by Stanley Kubrick.

Coming soon to a bookshop near you . . .

BARTON FINK and MILLER'S CROSSING

Straight from their triple success at Cannes, Joel Coen and Ethan Coen's latest film about a writer in Hollywood, together with the best gangster film of 1991, MILLER'S CROSSING.

LIEBESTRAUM

A dark and moody new thriller, starring Kim Novak, directed and written by Mike Figgis (INTERNAL AFFAIRS).

If you would like a Faber Film Books stocklist, then please write to:

> Faber and Faber Publishing Ltd
> 3 Queen Square
> London WC1N 3AU